NIGELLA EXPRESS

GOOD FOOD, FAST

Also by Nigella Lawson

HOW TO EAT
THE PLEASURES AND PRINCIPLES OF GOOD FOOD

HOW TO BE A DOMESTIC GODDESS
BAKING AND THE ART OF COMFORT COOKING

NIGELLA BITES
FROM FAMILY MEALS TO ELEGANT DINNERS — EASY, DELECTABLE RECIPES
FOR ANY OCCASION

FOREVER SUMMER

FEAST
FOOD THAT CELEBRATES LIFE

NIGELLA EXPRESS

GOOD FOOD, FAST

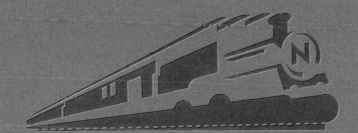

NIGELLA LAWSON

Photographs by Lis Parsons

HYPERION

DESIGN AND ART DIRECTION: CAZ HILDEBRAND
COOKERY ASSISTANT: HETTIE POTTER
EDITORIAL ASSISTANT: ZOE WALES
LAYOUT/DESIGN: JULIE MARTIN
ILLUSTRATIONS: WEST ONE ARTS & MARK PATON
INDEX: VICKI ROBINSON

ISBN: 978-1-4013-2243-4

HYPERION BOOKS ARE AVAILABLE FOR SPECIAL PROMOTIONS AND PREMIUMS.
FOR DETAILS CONTACT MICHAEL RENTAS, PROPRIETARY MARKETS, HYPERION, 77 WEST
66TH STREET, 12TH FLOOR, NEW YORK, NEW YORK 10023, OR CALL 212-456-0133.

FIRST EDITION

10 9 8 7 6 5 4 3 2 1

I am grateful to Elinor Klivans and her publisher, Chronicle Books,
San Francisco, for permission to reprint her recipe for
Totally Chocolate Chocolate Chip Cookies
from her book *Big Fat Cookies*.

CONTENTS

INTRODUCTION

This is, as the title makes clear, a book about fast food, but it is a book about fast food for those who love eating. Perhaps that's self-evident: How could I write any other sort? But I start with this premise because so much is written about the need to reduce the time we must spend cooking, it's as if the kitchen were a hateful place, almost an unsafe place, and that it must be only reasonable for us to avoid it. I love food, I adore being in the kitchen and I am happy to cook. But here's the problem: The day doesn't have enough gaps in it for me to do much shopping and the evening — what with the battles over homework, the still unchecked-off list of things I was meant to do, the calls I was supposed to return — doesn't yield much time to cook. But I must eat, and I must eat well — or else what is the point of it all? And then there are the people who need to be fed. I don't mention them grudgingly, either. I love to feed people, and rare is the person who comes into my home and leaves without a foil parcel of something from the kitchen.

I have had to adapt. I manage to have a fridge full of food and a life rich in the expectation of dinner, but within the confines of a timetable that is disorganized, busy, full of things I want to do as well as things I don't want to do — though sometimes I'm so tired I can't tell the difference. In short, I have a normal life, the sort we all share. To be sure, I can occasionally find the odd weekend or rainy afternoon when I am able to lose myself in an afternoon's stirring, chopping, kneading, or general pursuit of unhurried cooking, but for the most part, I am either in a hurry or in some state of psycho-fizz or obligation-overload, and food has to be fitted in.

Even if I might never have thought that a book of fast food recipes would be the natural one for me to write, it has been both

pleasurable and easy. After all, the recipes are already there. For this is the food I do eat, day in day out. I don't know if I have quite spelled out my food obsessiveness before, but it's the case that I take notes of everything I cook (even if the notes are sometimes hard to read later), and I keep a digital camera in the kitchen to record each finished dish, if not for posterity, for my own greedy archives. In a way, then, this book has written itself. This is just as well, since I left myself barely enough time to write it. My sister, Horatia, said I was like Wallace and Gromit, laying down the tracks just in time for the train to ride over them; and although it's been a bit hairy at times, it does, however, seem entirely fitting for a book called *Nigella Express*.

I feel, though, that I must emphasize this: Cooking is only one part of the exercise; the shopping and planning can be the most stressful parts. I have tried to keep the ingredients lists as short as possible and, although I haven't excluded all recondite items from them, I try to make sure any shopping trip pays for itself, timewise. That's to say, if I ask you (or myself) to buy something for one recipe, I try to supply other outings for it. But avoiding the recherché or unfamiliar wouldn't be the answer, in any case: after all, there is no way, however basic the supplies required, that shopping can be dispensed with. Eggs and bacon don't magically appear in the kitchen: they need to be shopped for just as coconut milk or wasabi does. I make this embarrassingly obvious point, because I think we all need reminding of it.

It's not, however, for me to tell you how to plan your shopping or order your storecupboard. I do much of my shopping on the Internet (too much, some would say), go to specialty stores when I find the time (for me that's fun, not duty), and have the odd turn around the supermarket. In the occasional recipe, where I've thought it might be helpful, I've noted an online source for an ingredient that could be harder for you to find locally.

I've also been quite strict with myself. I can't — couldn't possibly — eradicate all witter from my writing life, but I have tried to restrict the babble to the introduction to each recipe and have then given the method in a number of short, precise steps. This is to make sure you never have to turn a page to continue a recipe and to help every step read as clearly as it can. There isn't a recipe in here that isn't gloriously simple to cook, and I wanted to make that immediately evident on the page.

I could go on, but in the interest of brevity and the *Express* spirit, it seems only right to cut straight to the chase. The recipes that follow are not simply quick to cook, they attempt to make the whole of your cooking life — and as a consequence all of your life — easier. They are arranged in chapters, but please don't feel confined by these. Read, browse, sample, fiddle about as you see fit. As in cooking, so in life: We muddle through as best we can and this is what *Nigella Express* is all about.

NOTE FOR THE READER

• ALL EGGS ARE LARGE, ORGANIC

• ALL BUTTER IS UNSALTED

• ALL HERBS ARE FRESH, UNLESS STATED

• ALL CHOCOLATE IS DARK (MIN. 70% COCOA SOLIDS), UNLESS STATED

• SEE PAGE 353 FOR INFORMATION ABOUT INFUSED OILS

Most days, I approach cooking supper with less than absolute perkiness. This is never because I can't face it or even that I resent it, but because, at the end of a long, working day, and after I have wrestled with children's homework and other domestic demands, and feel that I am nothing more than the sum of my impatience and irritation and, of course, tetchy exhaustion, I just can't even think of what there might be to cook.

Actually, the cooking itself is the least of it, and this is not just because the kitchen is a place of sanctuary for me. Now, planning, shopping, deciding: These are the real drainers. I sometimes think how much easier things were in my grandmother's day. She had a schedule, and an unchanging one. Without looking at a calendar, I could know what day of the week it was by what I was given for dinner there. Of course, we are more adventurous these days and would not wish to inflict that tedium on our children. But a little of that order is desirable. I actually think it can lead to more variation rather than less. I don't like to own up to how often my children get pasta with pesto or meat sauce for supper because I am accustomed to life as a free spirit in the kitchen.

So now what I try and do is make sure that I am a little more repetitive than I once might have liked while writing my shopping lists. Luckily, I begin to see that repetition, too, has its virtues. I know, at least, that I can get supper on the table without going shopping afresh every day. I don't follow the recipes below enormously rigorously; that's to say I certainly deviate, both in the regularity with which they appear and the irregularity of the way in which I follow them. I am not good at authority, even when that authority is my own.

Still, I have one rule and it's a simple enough one to adhere to. And it's that it's never worth cooking anything for supper unless it can stand on equal footing with one of life's great and simplest gastro-delights, boiled egg on toast (the best free-range eggs, soft boiled, rapidly peeled and squished on thick sourdough or rye toast). Of course, I don't want that every day, but nor do I want to settle for anything less. If it can't measure up to that, I don't want to eat it. However little time or effort I can expend on the day's supper, I have to know it will deliver nothing less than pure pleasure. The recipes that follow satisfy that most necessary of edicts.

SMOKED COD AND CANNELLINI

Of all my reliable standbys, this is one of my speediest. Of course there's more to it. I'm too greedy to settle for mere efficiency. I first made this with some smoked haddock which I'd been thinking of using for a kedgeree, but I ran out of steam — and time. My thinking was that replacing the starch of the rice with the starch of some cannellini beans would work. It did. Indeed it worked so well, I can now never be without some canned cannellini in the cupboard.

Inspiration doesn't tell the whole story, as the dish that follows bears no relation at all to kedgeree, being rather more Italianate than Anglo-Indian in its flavor. The spontaneity of end-of-the-day cooking means — however I might mean to plan — that this is, in culinary terms, sui generis.

But then I take the view that most of the best things in life are happy accidents.

12 oz smoked cod (or haddock) fillet	2 14-oz cans/$3^1/_2$ cups cannellini
small sprig parsley including stalks	beans
2 bay leaves	$^1/_4$–$^1/_2$ cup fish-cooking liquid (see 3,
1 teaspoon peppercorns	below)
1 celery stalk	2 tablespoons extra virgin olive oil
$1^2/_3$ cups water	2 tablespoons chopped parsley
$^1/_3$ cup white wine	1 tablespoon chopped chives, optional

1 Lay the fish fillets in a large frying pan with the sprig of parsley, bay leaves, peppercorns, and celery stalk. Pour in the water and wine and bring to a boil.

2 Cover the pan with foil and simmer the fish in the poaching liquid for 3–5 minutes, depending on the thickness of the fish. Take off the heat and remove the fish, wrapping the pieces in foil to keep warm.

3 Tip out all but about $^1/_4$–$^1/_2$ cup of the poaching liquid from the pan. This will depend on the depth of your pan.

4 Drain the canned beans, rinsing them in a sieve or colander to get rid of any gloopiness and add to the pan, warming them in the poaching liquid for about 3 minutes. (Add a little more poaching liquid if necessary to moisten the beans.)

5 Turn off the heat and place the fish on top of the beans in the pan. Add the oil, most of the parsley, and the chives, if you're using them, stirring everything together, breaking up the fish as you go.

6 Check the seasoning and turn out into a couple of bowls or plates, sprinkle with a last bit of parsley, and eat, with relish.

Serves 2

ANGLO-ASIAN LAMB SALAD

I love the tangy fire of Thai cooking; I love equally the traditional English partnership of lamb with red currant and mint. I just happened, one day, just because of what I had in the kitchen, to bring the two together. Consider it an ovine reworking of those hot and sour beef salads of Southeast Asia. A lamb loin, sometimes described as the eye of the saddle, is the fleshy component, though any lean cut of lamb would do. Red currant jelly stands in for the sweetness of jaggery or palm sugar and I use rice vinegar (always easily on hand) instead of lime juice. I am not married to someone who would normally regard a salad as a treat for supper, but my husband loves this — and doesn't even notice it is a salad.

It is also a useful recipe to have up your sleeve for a starter on days when dining seems to require one. I try and keep those days — or nights — to a minimum, or to when I'm in a restaurant.

2 teaspoons garlic-infused oil
1 loin of lamb, approx. 8 oz in weight
2 tablespoons fish sauce (nam pla)
2 tablespoons rice vinegar
1 tablespoon red currant jelly
1 teaspoon soy sauce

1 red chile, deseeded and finely chopped, or $1/4$ teaspoon dried chile flakes
1 scallion, finely sliced
4 cups salad leaves
3 tablespoons freshly chopped mint

1 Heat the garlic-infused oil in a pan, and cook the lamb for 5 minutes on one side, turning it over and cooking for another $2^1/2$ minutes on the other. Wrap the meat in foil, making a baggy package that is a tightly sealed parcel, and let it rest for about 5 minutes.

2 In a medium-sized bowl, whisk together the fish sauce, vinegar, red currant jelly, soy sauce, deseeded chopped chile, and sliced scallion.

3 Open the foil parcel, emptying the meat juices into the dressing. Slice the lamb into very fine slices or strips and add them too; the acid in the dressing will "cook" the lamb a little more while it is steeped. If it is not very rare, I'd leave it for a short time and, consequently, for a longer time if it seems undercooked. You want it still gorgeously pink on its salad.

4 Divide the salad leaves among two (or four) plates and then arrange the lamb with the dressing over each one. Finally, scatter over the chopped mint.

Serves 2 as a main course, 4 as a starter

SALMON ESCALOPES WITH WATERCRESS, SUGAR SNAPS, AND AVOCADO

This is an ideal recipe for those days when you're as squeezed for time to shop as to cook: You just rush in to the supermarket at lunch or on the way home, grab a few packages, and rush out again.

"Wok oil" is how the oil I like to use here comes labeled: It contains vegetable oil, sesame oil, ginger, and garlic; but garlic oil, chile oil or, indeed, just oil-oil would be fine.

2 thin-cut salmon steaks or escalopes, approx. 4 oz each
2 tablespoons rice vinegar
1 teaspoon sugar
$\frac{1}{2}$ teaspoon kosher salt or $\frac{1}{4}$ teaspoon table salt

2 tablespoons wok oil
4 cups watercress
1 cup miniature sugar snap peas
1 small ripe avocado

1 Heat a heavy-based, nonstick skillet and when hot cook the salmon escalopes for about a minute a side. Remove to a couple of dinner plates.

2 Whisk the rice vinegar, sugar, salt, and wok oil together and drizzle each salmon steak with about a teaspoon each, and set the rest aside for a moment.

3 Divide the watercress and sugar snaps between each plate and then halve the avocado, remove the stone, and, using a teaspoon, gouge out the avocado flesh, dropping the pieces as you go in amongst the tangle of watercress and sugar snaps.

4 Pour the remaining dressing over the salads and serve immediately.

Serves 2

MUSTARD PORK CHOPS

I love the old French favorites, the sorts that evoke not the supercilious waiter and theatrically removed silvered dome of the big-name restaurants, but rather the small-town bistro, all warm wood and rough red wine.

This is possibly the easiest route to a proper, filling, and yet strangely delicate dinner. The pork is cooked for just enough time to take away pinkness but ensure tenderness within, and gloriously scorched without. The mustard, cider, and cream add comfort and piquancy.

To soak up the gorgeous juices, and to serve as a fantastically quick potato substitute, I serve up gnocchi alongside. You could always add a little lemony fennel, sliced thinly, or a green salad if you're in the mood.

2 pork chops, about 1 lb total weight
2 teaspoons garlic oil
1/2 cup hard cider

1 tablespoon whole-grain mustard
1/3 cup heavy cream

1 Cut the fat off the chops, and then bash them briefly but brutally with a rolling pin between two pieces of plastic wrap to make them thinner.

2 Heat the oil in a pan, and then cook the chops over a moderately high heat for about 5 minutes per side. Remove them to a warmed plate.

3 Pour the cider into the pan, still over the heat, to deglaze the pan. Let it bubble away for a minute or so, then add the mustard and stir in the cream.

4 Let the sauce continue cooking for a few minutes before pouring over each plated pork chop. If you're having gnocchi with, make sure you turn them in the pan to absorb any spare juices before adding them to your plates.

Serves 2

Turkey Fillets with Anchovy, Gherkin, and Dill

I have long been an excitable fan of turkey, that's to say the familiar festive roast turkey, but I have come only recently to appreciate the blander, leaner cuts that line our supermarkets' refrigerated shelves. Do I sound sneering? Force of habit, perhaps. I have long resisted the sort of meat that is prized almost exclusively for its low fat content (what a thing to do, to like food for what it lacks), but I've found myself cooking with turkey parts more and more. Not least, I love the contrast of its mild meat to sharp, pungent flavorings, the sort of flavorings that live by my stove and lend themselves to lazy evening cooking very handsomely.

The saltiness of the anchovies and the sharpness of the gherkins give the timid turkey real bite here, and I love the Germanic sprinkling of dill after. I tend to eat this with something plain, rice from the rice cooker or some steamed tiny new potatoes or a vast plate of broccoli. The broccoli (in this case some fabulous sprouting purple broccoli) needs no more than some butter or oil, but if you feel like going all out (relatively speaking), try the mustard-caper butter sauce on the facing page.

5 anchovy fillets
2 tablespoons olive oil
14 oz/3 small turkey breast fillets, beaten as thinly as possible, each fillet then cut in half

2 tablespoons vermouth
2 gherkins, finely chopped
2 tablespoons chopped fresh dill

1 Heat the anchovy fillets and oil in a frying pan, stirring with a wooden spoon until the fillets begin to melt in the pan.

2 Flash-fry the turkey in the same pan, cooking for a couple of minutes on each side. Remove the meat to a warm serving plate.

3 Add the vermouth and chopped gherkins, and let the liquid reduce and sizzle for a minute or so.

4 Pour over the plated turkey and sprinkle with the chopped dill.

Serves 4

MUSTARD-CAPER SAUCE FOR BROCCOLI

6 tablespoons butter
2 teaspoons Dijon mustard

juice of half a lemon
2 tablespoons capers

1 Put the butter, mustard, and lemon juice into a pan over medium heat.

2 As the butter melts, whisk all the ingredients together and then add the capers.

3 Pour the emulsified sauce over cooked broccoli and serve.

Makes enough to dress $1/2$ to 1 lb broccoli

RED SHRIMP AND MANGO CURRY

This is one of the easiest suppers to make and somehow, however much I know this, it always surprises me. Not in the cooking, so much as in the eating: I can't believe, each time anew, how deep and textured and full-throttle, in a sweet, comforting way, this tastes, when all I did was a bit of shopping and some light stirring.

Obviously it helps if you can have some of the convenience stuff I list below: The peeled and cubed squash, sweet potato, and mango I find at the supermarket make this a breeze. But if you can't find them, no matter: Add some drained canned chickpeas and perhaps, for some sour-sweet edge, some pineapple that's been in its own juice, not syrup. As for the coconut milk, I often use the whole can rather than a mere half below; it really depends on whether I feel like eating out of a deep bowl, soupily, or a shallow one. To go with I suggest either plain rice or some plain wide rice noodles cooked according to package instructions (all of about 2 minutes) and tossed in some toasted chopped unsalted coconut-flavored peanuts.

If you have some fresh shrimp so much the better, but I stipulate the frozen ones below since I regularly keep them in the freezer for an evening when I feel like eating gorgeously with very little forethought.

1 scallion, finely sliced	12 oz/2^1/$_2$ cups butternut squash and
1 tablespoon garlic or chile oil	sweet potato cubes
1^1/$_2$ tablespoons red Thai curry paste	7 oz frozen king shrimp to give 2 cups
(or according to taste)	1 cup mango cubes
about half of a 14-oz can coconut milk	1 teaspoon lime juice
to give 1 cup	3–4 tablespoons chopped fresh
1 cup chicken stock	cilantro
2 teaspoons fish sauce (nam pla)	

1 Fry the sliced scallion in the oil for a minute, then add the curry paste.

2 Whisk in the coconut milk, stock, and fish sauce and bring to a boil.

3 Tip in the butternut squash and sweet potato cubes and simmer, partially covered, for about 15 minutes or until tender.

4 Drain the shrimp under running water to remove excess ice and tumble them into the pan, letting the sauce come back to a boil. When it does, add the diced mango and lime juice and cook for another minute or so until the shrimp are cooked through.

5 Sprinkle with the chopped cilantro as you serve over plain rice or wide rice noodles, or even both.

Serves 2–4, depending on hunger and whether you're expecting to eat anything else at supper.

QUICK CALAMARI WITH GARLIC MAYONNAISE

Strange though it might sound to say it, this is another of my supper standbys. I keep the frozen calamari in the deep-freeze, taking it out in the morning at breakfast to let it thaw in time for the evening's meal. I prefer to eat a massive amount of this, and nothing else (I can eat the whole lot myself) rather than have it more meanly as a starter unless, in a life outside of this chapter's parameters, I'm expecting company, in which case it would happily stretch to four people, ready to dunk each crisp piece of squid into the garlic mayonnaise over pre-dinner drinks.

1 cup peanut oil or as needed
   depending on the size of pan
1 lb frozen calamari (tubes and
   tentacles) to give 12 oz unfrozen,
   thawed in the refrigerator
$1/4$ cup semolina
2 tablespoons cornstarch
2 teaspoons Old Bay seasoning (or
   use salt and paprika)

FOR THE GARLIC MAYONNAISE
1 clove garlic
$1/2$ cup best quality, preferably
   organic, mayonnaise

1 Heat the oil in a smallish saucepan and while it's heating, cut the thawed calamari into $1/2$- inch rings.

2 Put the semolina, cornstarch, and seasoning into a plastic freezer bag.

3 Add the calamari rings and tentacles and then toss to coat.

4 When the oil is hot enough, which is when it sizzles up fiercely when you drop in a small cube of bread, fry the calamari in batches to get the most golden crunchiness. A couple of minutes per batch is all you should need.

5 Lift the calamari from the pan using a slotted spoon and drain on paper towels.

6 Grate or crush the garlic. Stir well to mix into the mayonnaise and serve alongside the fried calamari.

Serves 2

Naan Pizza

At times when I'm pretending to indulge the children, but am really too exhausted to cook, I order pizza. But actually this is my preferred option. I can eat a whole pizza in its box and always regret it afterward. This is not much harder to cook than making a phone call and I feel much happier for it. This is my topping of preference; feel free to play about to make your own. All I feel strongly is that while takeout pizza crusts are vile, packaged naans, when heated, are not.

1 naan, about 8 inches long
2 teaspoons tomato puree (chopped and sieved tomatoes) from a jar or other tomato sauce

$^1/_2$ cup drained mixed mushroom antipasto from a jar
$^1/_2$ cup roughly chopped fontina
3 fresh thyme stalks

1 Preheat the oven to 425°F. Lay the naan on a baking sheet lined with baking parchment, aluminum foil, or a Silpat.

2 Spread tomato puree or sauce over the naan, then tumble over the drained mushrooms and sprinkle over the chopped cheese before finally strewing with the thyme leaves stripped from the stalks.

3 Cook in the oven for about 5 minutes, by which time the cheese should be bubbling and melted. Be careful not to burn your mouth.

Serves 1

ROAST CORNISH HEN AND SWEET POTATOES

This is my almost regular as clockwork Saturday night supper. I find it enormously easy and relaxing to make since all I do is go downstairs, put everything in the oven, and then go back up to Saturday evening TV in bed until it's ready — and then, frankly, back again.

If I cook the Cornish hens in the same pan as the sweet potatoes, I cut a couple of slices of bread and put one underneath each bird in the pan, so as to absorb the juices and stop them from seeping into the sweet potatoes, which, in turn, would prevent them from crisping and browning. But more often than not, I dispense with the bread (you can imagine how good it tastes later though) and just get two disposable foil roasting pans about the size of brownie pans each and put the Cornish hens in one and the sweet potatoes in another and reunite on the plate with a little watercress and a squirt of lime juice later.

I must have English mustard with this. I know it's a weakness, but not one I'm willing to renounce.

2 Cornish hens
2 tablespoons garlic or canola oil
1 sweet potato, weighing
  approximately 1 lb
$^1/_4$ teaspoon ground cumin

$^1/_4$ teaspoon ground cinnamon
1–2 bunches of watercress
kosher salt
good squirt lime juice

1 Preheat the oven to 425°F. Put the birds into a small baking pan or foil pan, pouring over 1 tablespoon of oil.

2 Cut the unpeeled sweet potato into $2^1/_2$-inch cubes and put them into another smallish pan or foil pan.

3 Pour over the other tablespoon of oil and sprinkle over the spices, then toss everything together by shaking the pan.

4 Cook both the hens and sweet potatoes in the preheated oven for 45 minutes.

5 Put each Cornish hen on a plate, with a tangle of watercress and the sweet potatoes alongside. Sprinkle with kosher salt to taste and spritz with lime juice, and go to it!

Serves 2

CARAMEL CROISSANT PUDDING

I always think that some of the best recipes come from the thrifty refusal to throw any-thing away. Certainly I made this one Monday evening because I had two stale croissants left over from the weekend and just knew they could be put to good use. Now, adding cream and bourbon is probably a lot less thrifty than throwing some stale bread away in the first place, but this is such a fabulous dessert that I now think it should be every Monday night's supper. And I mean supper: With something this substantial, you certainly need eat nothing beforehand. Though I admit a small crunchy salad may not be a bad idea first.

Oh, and if you don't have any bourbon in the house, first may I say, please con-sider it, and second, replace it, rather, with rum. Scotch whisky may seem the obvious substitute but it would be the wrong one, I feel.

2 stale croissants	$1/2$ cup whole milk
1 cup sugar	2 tablespoons bourbon
2 tablespoons water	2 eggs, beaten
$1/2$ cup heavy cream	

1 Preheat the oven to 350°F.

2 Tear the croissants into pieces and put in a small gratin dish; I use a cast-iron oval one with a capacity of about 2 cups for this.

3 Put the sugar and water into a saucepan, and swirl around to help dissolve the sugar before putting the saucepan on the burner over medium to high heat.

4 Caramelize the sugar and water mixture by letting it bubble away until it all turns a deep amber color; this will take 3–5 minutes. Keep looking but don't be too timid.

5 Turn heat down to low and add the cream — ignoring all spluttering — and, whisking, the milk and bourbon. Any solid toffee that forms in the pan will dissolve easily if you keep whisking over low heat. Take off the heat and, still whisking, add the beaten eggs. Pour the caramel bourbon custard over the croissants and leave to steep for 10 minutes if the croissants are very stale.

6 Place in the preheated oven for 20 minutes and prepare to swoon.

Serves 2 greedy people

Rhubarb and Custard Gelato

Everyday Easy

There is no variation on rhubarb and custard I don't love, and this is probably one of the easiest to make. You buy some good eggy vanilla ice cream and make a stovetop compote — very quick, and gorgeous poured warm over the ice cream with the rest chilled in the fridge and eaten with yogurt for breakfast.

1 lb rhubarb (untrimmed)
$3/_4$ cup sugar
2 tablespoons best-quality pure vanilla extract
A few scoops of ice cream (for two people)

1 Cut the rhubarb into $1/_4$-inch slices, discarding the leaves and tough ends.

2 Put all of the ingredients except the ice cream into a saucepan and bring to a boil, stirring as the pan heats up to help dissolve the sugar.

3 Partially cover the pan and simmer for about 3 minutes, then uncover completely and cook for another couple of minutes, or until the rhubarb is soft and melting into the pink syrup. though still keeping its shape — just.

4 Pour into a pitcher and leave to cool a little.

Makes approximately 2 cups, which is enough for a good 6 portions, but feel happy — please — to use as much as you like.

BUTTERSCOTCH FRUIT FONDUE

If ever you've — lazily, guiltily — bought peeled, sliced, cubed fruit from the super-market and then wondered why you bothered, as you get home to discover the fruit is brightly hued but dimly flavored, this is the solution. Anything, frankly, dunked into a butterscotch sauce tastes good, and this is a fabulous everyday or even party dessert.

I own up, the fruit in the picture did come out of a cellophane package, the mango already cubed, the melon sliced, but mostly I make this for the children using bananas and pears I have actually managed to peel and slice myself. The strawberries you don't even need to hull: Their stalks are useful to lower the berries into the molten fondue.

I give everyone — here just the two of us — a little cup of fondue for their own individual dipping. It does mean you make more sauce than is needed, but it gets around the shared spit and saliva issue. Or you could make half the amount and pour it over the mix of cubed pineapple, papaya, and mango.

Either way, you don't want the butterscotch fondue too fiercely hot, not least because it will be too runny. If you make it before you sit down to eat altogether, it should be just about perfect by the time you reach dessert. I am also pretty keen on this cold, spooned straight from the cup.

You could substitute dark corn syrup for the golden syrup, but I'm afraid it doesn't have the viscosity or flavor. Since you can now get Lyle's Golden Syrup sent to you from Amazon Gourmet, I don't feel bad recommending the less familiar ingredient.

3 tablespoons light brown sugar	1/2 cup heavy cream
2 tablespoons granulated sugar	splash of pure vanilla extract
1/2 cup golden syrup	approx. 12 oz cut fruit
2 tablespoons butter	

1 Melt the sugars, syrup, and butter in a saucepan and boil for 5 minutes.

2 Add the cream and vanilla, stirring together, and then take off the heat.

3 Divide the sauce between two cups or small bowls, and then arrange the fruit on two saucers or on a plate, as you see fit.

Serves 2

WORKDAY WINNERS

There are few things so likely to put a strain onto the working day as knowing you've got people coming over for supper a few minutes after you've walked through the front door, let alone taken your coat off. I don't wish to sound negative. I do, it's true, have a tendency toward slight hermit-like cocooning, especially in the winter, but I also love to be in a room full of friends in the evening. And if I think about it, most of the time when I do have people over for supper, it is during the week. Weekends can get so taken over by my children's social life, there really isn't any time for my own. But that suits me. One of the good things about a midweek supper party is that no one expects the grand treatment. And I always, always prefer the mood to be informal.

So make life easier on yourself by dispensing with a starter. I know I've said this before, but it bears repetition. It's not just that you don't want the extra cooking, but neither do you want an extra course's worth of washing up. And I don't think you want dinner to be an overlong affair. It may not sound hospitable, but who wants a really late night in the middle of the working week?

Only have a starter if it makes life easier for you. Sometimes it can help to have some food for people to pick at over a drink or two: It means you can get on with getting supper together calmly, and keeps everyone happy. I also think sometimes it makes sense to balance the amount of food you have to put on the table. So, by giving a first course, maybe you can provide just a salad with the main course, and not potatoes too — that sort of thing. Sometimes I use a bit of starter action to make me feel less guilty about giving everyone roast chicken *again*. And you don't actually have to cook the starter; a few bits and pieces thrown together is all you need — like the shrimp and harissa dip or crab salad that follow, for obvious example.

And you can take the lack of effort further, without feeling bad about it at all. A bit of judicious — and pleasurable if you're lucky — shopping and you don't have to do a thing. I buy some salami, uncut and still in sausage form, as well as some sliced and arrange them with a knife or two on a wooden board. Parmesan bought in a wedge and then cut into crumbly hunks is another labor-light way of going about feeding people when they arrive. Slighter higher up the effort scale, but only a tiny bit, is to buy some frozen edamame beans from a store that deals in Japanese foodstuffs. These are soybeans in the pod, which you boil for about five minutes from frozen and then sprinkle lavishly if unfashionably with rock salt before being podded, their jade beans popped into the mouth, while still warm.

Buy a tub of hummus, mix it with half its volume of Greek yogurt, stir in a little ground cumin and grated lemon zest, drizzle with olive oil and scatter with pomegranate seeds, and serve with breadsticks or sliced pita. Or buy a good tub of lemony (preferably organic) mayonnaise and grate in a little garlic and set an array of raw vegetables on the table to be dipped into it. If you can't face chopping vegetables, then go heavy on sugar snaps instead.

Above all, be relaxed. I know it's always an irritating injunction, but this should be a supper with friends, around a table, with you able to enjoy them. Food always helps, but even a dinner gone wrong can be a great evening. And once you accept that mistakes in the kitchen don't need to matter, you're less likely to make them in the first place. Anyway, none of the recipes that follow should give either the novice or the merely tired any cause for culinary, or other, concern.

SHRIMP WITH MARYAM ZAIRA SAUCE

OK, so this is the idea: Sauce Marie Rose goes Moroccan. Instead of the usual tomato ketchup (well, be honest) I dollop in some good store-bought harissa. It works wonderfully, and the honey makes up for the sugar you lack by giving up the Heinz. Be careful when you buy harissa though, as not only does it vary enormously in strength but also some jars that bear the name are not really harissa but some paste made red with beetroot and carrot. Check the back of the jar for ingredients. I used a gorgeously mild harissa here, a rose harissa, that I find poetically desirable. But start with a small amount of the harissa you've got before working up to the amount I have stipulated below.

I love shrimp with their shells still on; a bit of DIY at the table always seems to help the atmosphere. But if you hate mess and can't bear the sight of seeing people dropping shells all over the place and haven't got time for treatment, then simply buy peeled shrimp instead.

1 cup good store-bought, preferably organic, mayonnaise	1 teaspoon lime juice
	1 teaspoon honey
1/4 cup harissa	1 lb cooked shell-on cooked shrimp

1 Mix together all the sauce ingredients, and put into a bowl for dipping.

2 Arrange the shrimp on a plate for people to pluck, peel, and dip into the sauce, making sure you have enough in the way of plates or saucers dotted about the place for detritus.

Serves 4–6

CRAB AND AVOCADO SALAD WITH JAPANESE DRESSING

This is another one of those salads that my husband doesn't notice is a salad and that we eat fairly often at home. Now that I can find good, fresh tubs of crabmeat at the supermarket I can really rely on this as a table and tummy filler when I don't have much time for slow, store-by-specialty-store shopping. The quantities below provide generous amounts for four people, so this is the sort of starter that you can use to save you coming up with enormous amounts later on in the evening. I often halve it for a quick supper for the two of us at home, or when it's me and a girlfriend and a chilled bottle of rosé.

2 tablespoons mirin
1 tablespoon rice vinegar
$1/2$ teaspoon wasabi paste
$1/2$ teaspoon kosher salt or $1/4$
    teaspoon regular salt
few drops sesame oil
1 long red chile pepper, deseeded and
    finely chopped

$1^1/_4$ cups cooked crabmeat
approx. 1 teaspoon lime juice
5 cups arugula or other tender, dark
    green salad leaves
1 ripe avocado
1–2 teaspoons chopped chives

1 In a bowl that will hold the crabmeat later, whisk together the mirin, rice vinegar, wasabi, salt, and sesame oil. Then remove around 4 teaspoons to another bowl large enough for the salad later.

2 To the first, more generous amount of dressing add the finely chopped chile and then the crabmeat, and fork through to mix thoroughly.

3 To the small amount of dressing in the other bowl, add the lime juice and then the salad leaves and toss well to mix before arranging on four plates.

4 Spoon a quarter of the crab mixture into a regular metal kitchen $1/_3$-cup measure, squishing down to get it all in, then take it over to a salad-lined plate and unmold in the center of it. Just turn over, tap, and the crabmeat should fall out. Continue with the remaining three quarters of the crabmeat and the three other plates.

5 Using a rounded half teaspoon measure, scoop out curls or humps of avocado and dot around on top of the salady bits. Spritz with a little lime juice.

6 Sprinkle the chopped chives over the four mounds of crab and take the plates to the table.

Serves 4 as a starter

SAKE SEA BASS AND WILTED GREENS

This is very calm, very plain, very good. It's what I make for people on diets or who don't like anything too vigorous or when I feel in need of a Zen moment. I am aware that doesn't make it sound very exciting, but fresh fish doesn't need anything to make it exciting, it just needs to be allowed to be tasted. And this is the sort of elegant, pared-down food that's hard to get in a restaurant. If you want to have potatoes with, then steam some (this will take longer than the fish, but requires no effort).

Easier though, to provide a little something first and make everyone happy with the confident restraint of just fabulous fish and some flavorsome wilted greens.

2 sea bass, approx. 2 lb	2 tablespoons soy sauce
4 scallions	1 teaspoon grated fresh ginger
6 tablespoons sake	

1 Preheat the oven to 400°F. Lay each sea bass on a large piece of foil, and bring up the sides ready to make a parcel.

2 Slice the scallions in half lengthwise and place 4 pieces into the cavity of each fish.

3 Sprinkle 3 tablespoons of sake into each parcel, 1 tablespoon of soy, and about half a teaspoon of the grated ginger into each.

4 Wrap the parcels loosely but sealed firmly, and cook on a baking sheet for about 25 minutes.

5 Open the cooked fish parcels, peel away the skin from the top of each fish, and fillet the top layer of fish.

6 Turn the fish over, repeat the same process, and then spoon over any juices from the parcel onto the filleted sea bass and serve with the wilted greens.

Serves 4–6

WILTED GREENS

I use anything on hand: bok choy torn up small, snow peas, spinach, assorted bits from the bottom of the vegetable drawer and salad compartment. This is *the* best way I've found of using up bags and bits of designer leaves that are past their best — not bad, but no longer beautiful enough to be served as salad.

    2 tablespoons garlic-infused oil
    2 anchovy fillets
    12 cups assorted green vegetables

1 Heat the oil and anchovies in a wok or large pan and stir until the anchovies seem to start melting into the oil.

2 Toss in your green veg and stir-fry over fairly high heat — a few minutes at the most — until everything has wilted.

Serves 4

BRANDIED-BACONY CHICKEN

I've never made a secret of my love and respect for a plain, old-fashioned, unreconstructed roast chicken. Why would I? But sometimes it's good to play, and the brandy and bacon here bring flavor (and help the bird bronze up beautifully) but not distraction. It's still what it is.

Alongside, I serve the potato and mushroom gratin that follows and a lemony, crunchy green salad, *et c'est tout*. And if you want to dispense with the potato element altogether, I suggest this almost effort-free substitution: simply drain two cans of puy lentils, and when the chicken is roasted, and standing on a carving tray, warm up the lentils in the hot chickeny juices in the tin and serve as they are, sprinkled with parsley if you feel so inclined.

This is not speedy-speedy in actual cooking time but it's fantastically helpful when you have people for supper since all it requires is about 10 minutes prep, and then you can set the table, have a drink, and put on lipstick while everything cooks happily by itself in a hot oven.

1 chicken approx. 2$^1/_2$–3 lbs
2 strips bacon
$^1/_4$ cup brandy

1 Heat the oven to 425°F.

2 In a small skillet cook the bacon over medium heat until it's crisp and the pan full of gorgeous bacony fat, about 4 minutes.

3 Take the pan off the heat, the bacon out of the pan and straight into the cavity of the chicken, sitting the chicken in a roasting pan as you do so, breast side up.

4 Pour the brandy into the still-hot frying pan with the bacon fat and let bubble for a minute then pour it over the chicken.

5 Roast for 45 minutes, making sure the juices run clear between leg and body. Let rest 10 minutes before carving.

Serves 4

POTATO AND MUSHROOM GRATIN

There are few sights as uplifting in the kitchen as a golden, bubbling gratin coming out of the oven, and this is the perfect accompaniment to the chicken, so everyone's happy. It's strange to be saying this, but one of the reasons I love this particular gratin is that it isn't too creamy and rich. And the relative thinness of the wine and milk the potatoes and mushrooms are cooked in — relative to heavy cream, that is — is what allows you to cook this in such a hot oven and so quickly.

The first two times I cooked this, I peeled the potatoes; now I don't bother. It isn't necessary (and I buy baking potatoes that come all clean and shiny) and even if peeling them doesn't really take long, it's a good psychological step to remove: this is now a quick slice and chop, in a pan and thence to the oven. It feels easy — but then it may be because it *is* easy.

3 average-sized/1¹/₂ lbs baking
   potatoes, thinly sliced
1¹/₂ cups milk
3 tablespoons white wine
salt and pepper to taste

2 tablespoons butter
2 teaspoons garlic-infused oil
8 oz cremini mushrooms, finely sliced
   to make 4 cups

1 Heat the oven to 425°F and butter a shallow baking dish or gratin.

2 Bring the sliced potatoes, milk, wine, salt, and pepper to a boil in a saucepan, stirring occasionally, and leave at a simmer while you get on with the mushrooms.

3 Melt the butter and garlic oil in a skillet over medium-high heat. Add the mushrooms and cook, stirring occasionally, until softened, about 3 minutes.

4 Pour the mushrooms and their garlicky, buttery juices into the pan of potatoes, stir to mix, and pour straight into the gratin dish. Bake for 45 minutes alongside the chicken or until piping hot, and crisp on top.

Serves 4

STEAK SLICE WITH LEMON AND THYME

This recipe, or rather the method, was suggested to me by my agent Ed Victor, and so is known familiarly as Ed's Tender Rump. The method is this: Instead of marinating the meat before cooking, you marinate it *after* — and it really does keep it extraordinarily tender. Please feel free to play around with the herbs; I rather think Ed himself uses oregano rather than the thyme I love.

I love this with broccoli rabe or those leggy tenderstem broccoli. A couple of packages, lightly cooked and then drained and set in the marinade after the beef's out and sliced, is the most heavenly accompaniment. And I can't tell you how good both steak and broccoli rabe are cold later.

1 rump steak 1 inch thick weighing approx. 1¼ lbs	⅓ cup extra virgin olive oil
5 stalks thyme to give 1 tablespoon stripped leaves	zest and juice of ½ lemon
2 cloves garlic, bruised	1 teaspoon kosher salt or ½ teaspoon table salt
	good grinding of fresh pepper

1 Cut away the fat from around the edge of the steak while you heat a griddle or pan.

2 Brush the steak with a little olive or vegetable oil to prevent it from sticking to the griddle or pan, and then cook for 3 minutes a side plus 1 minute each side turned again (this gives you pretty griddle marks) for desirably rare meat; the lemon in the post hoc marinade "cooks" it a little more.

3 While the steak is cooking, place the thyme leaves, garlic, oil, lemon zest, juice, salt, and pepper in a wide shallow dish.

4 Once the steak is cooked, place it in the dish of marinade for 4 minutes a side, before removing it to a board and slicing thinly on the diagonal.

Serves 4

SEARED SALMON WITH SINGAPORE NOODLES

I know the list of ingredients is long, but a lot of this is stuff that will help you generally if it's part of your cupboard stash. If you don't want to go in for specialty shopping at all (I love it, and now can indulge myself online, too) then replace the tiny dried shrimp with about $1/2$ cup of small frozen (though thaw them first) shrimp. Sherry could be used instead of the Chinese cooking wine, though I should tell you that I get this very straight-forwardly from my local supermarket.

FOR THE SALMON:

2 teaspoons medium Madras curry powder

1 teaspoon sugar

$1/4$ teaspoon table salt

4 approx. 6–8-oz salmon fillets

1 tablespoon garlic-infused oil

1 Mix the curry powder, sugar, and salt in a wide, shallow dish and dredge the salmon in this, turning the pieces all over in the rub.

2 Heat a pan with the oil and cook the fillets on high heat for about 2–3 minutes a side, searing the sides of the fillets too if they are very thick.

Serves 4

FOR THE NOODLES:

8 oz vermicelli rice noodles

$1/2$ cup dried shrimp

$1/2$ cup Chinese cooking wine

1 tablespoon garlic-infused oil

2 cups finely sliced napa cabbage

1 cup baby whole corn, sliced into thin rounds

2 scallions, finely sliced

2 teaspoons medium Madras curry powder

1 teaspoon minced fresh ginger

1 cup chicken stock (from concentrate or bouillon cubes)

3 tablespoons soy sauce

2 cups bean sprouts

$1/4$ cup chopped fresh cilantro

1 Put the rice noodles into a bowl and cover with boiling water. Leave them to soak for 4 minutes and then drain them.

2 Soak the dried shrimp in the wine, then heat the oil in a wok and fry the lettuce, baby corn, and scallions for a few minutes.

3 Add the curry powder and minced ginger to the wok, and then the stock and soy. Pour in the shrimp with their wine and the drained, soaked noodles, tossing and shaking everything all together in the wok.

4 Finally stir in the bean sprouts and give a final toss before turning out into a bowl and sprinkling the cilantro over.

Serves 4

LAYERED SALAD WITH ROAST QUAIL

This started off life in my kitchen as a layered salad with cold chicken in the mix, but I felt that the juicy crunchiness of the salad, its glorious, bright simplicity didn't need to be fleshed out. Roast quail seemed to me to be in just the right register, and what's more ridiculously easy to deal with. If you want, you can cook them a little ahead, since they're good warm rather than hot. And if there is salad and quail left over, then take the meat off the little birds and toss it in the salad the next day. Serve with a pile of, preferably warm, flat breads and quite a few finger bowls.

juice of 1 lemon
1 teaspoon kosher salt or 1/2 teaspoon table salt
1/3 cup olive oil
2 teaspoons honey
1/2 teaspoon dried mint; dried thyme is also good
12 quail
About 1 lb romaine lettuce, sliced into 1/2-inch shreds to make 5 cups
1 bunch/1 cup radishes, trimmed and sliced into fine rounds

1/2 cucumber, partly peeled to give a stripy effect and cut into 1/2-inch chunks
1 red bell pepper, deseeded and cut into 1/2-inch chunks
seeds from half a pomegranate (1/3 cup seeds)
2 tablespoons chopped fresh mint leaves

1 Preheat the oven to 425°F. Put the lemon juice and salt into a jar, add the oil, honey, and dried mint, and then put on the lid and shake like mad.

2 Arrange the quail in probably a couple of roasting pans, and pour over half the jar of dressing, basting the baby birds well before they go in the oven.

3 Roast the quail for 30 minutes, and while they're cooking get on with the salad.

4 Layer the salad ideally into a straight-sided glass bowl, drizzling a little of the remaining half jar of dressing from the quail on each layer as follows: romaine, radish slices, cucumber chunks, red pepper, more lettuce, and then pomegranate seeds with the chopped mint sprinkled on top.

Serves 6–8

ETON MESS

There is no variation of this dessert I don't like, and I must have made several in my time. This one uses bottled, proper fresh pomegranate juice to encourage the strawberries to ooze out their fragrant summery juices. If you're making this with out-of-season strawberries, then you stand a chance of using freshly squeezed pomegranate juice, in which case, sprinkle some seeds on top of this voluptuous mound of meringue and berry-spiked cream.

4 cups strawberries	**2 cups whipping cream**
2 teaspoons vanilla or granulated sugar	**4 small packaged meringue nests**
2 teaspoons pomegranate juice	

1 Hull and chop the strawberries. Put into a bowl, add the sugar and pomegranate juice, and leave to macerate while you whip the cream.

2 Whip the cream in a large bowl until thick but still soft. Roughly crumble in 4 of the meringue nests — you will need chunks for texture as well as a little fine dust.

3 Take out about half a cupful of the chopped strawberries, and fold the meringued cream and the rest of the fruit mixture together.

4 Arrange on 4 serving plates or glasses or in a mound, and top each one with some of the remaining macerated strawberries.

Serves 4

CARIBBEAN CREAMS

This is a reworking of my grandmother's Barbados creams: We're going the way of the coconut and the banana. It's scarcely a fancy dessert, but sometimes I think it can be sweetly comforting to have something a little homespun, and almost from the nursery. This is not that far from that old favorite, bananas mashed with cream and brown sugar. Hard to beat, to be sure, but the coconut yogurt and rum certainly add a little something.

You need to make these the morning (or day before, if that feels easier) of the evening you want to eat them, but they take no more than 5 minutes to prepare. So they are very quick to make and you ease the burden on that short time after you get back from work in the evening.

$3/4$ cup coconut yogurt   1 banana
$3/4$ cup heavy cream   2 tablespoons dark brown sugar
1 tablespoon coconut rum, such as
    Malibu (optional)

1 Stir together the yogurt and cream with the rum, if you're using it, and whisk until slightly thickened.

2 Slice the banana and then divide the slices between 4 x $1/2$ cup ramekins to form a layer at the bottom of each one.

3 Spoon in the thickened yogurt and cream mixture, filling the ramekins equally.

4 Sprinkle about $1^1/2$ teaspoons of sugar over each ramekin, and then wrap them in plastic wrap and place in the fridge overnight or for the day.

Serves 4

FLOURLESS CHOCOLATE BROWNIES

However much people have eaten there is always, I've noticed, room for a brownie. This is a different kind of a brownie, most definitely for party-dessert, melting, fudgy, and damply rich. I compound these qualities by serving it with ice cream and dark chocolate sauce that follows but there is no need. Need is not really what we're talking about here, though, is it?

8 oz semisweet chocolate	3 eggs, beaten
1 cup (2 sticks) butter	1½ cups ground almonds
1 cup sugar	1 cup chopped walnuts
2 teaspoons vanilla extract	

1 Preheat the oven to 325°F. Melt the chocolate and butter gently over low heat in a heavy-bottomed saucepan.

2 Add the sugar and vanilla to the pan off the heat, and let it cool a little.

3 Beat the eggs into the pan with the ground almonds and walnut pieces. Turn into a 9-inch square baking pan or, most sensibly, use a foil one.

4 Bake for 25–30 minutes, by which time the top will have set but the mixture will still be gooey. Once cooler, cut carefully, four down, four across, into 16 squidgy-bellied squares.

Makes 16 squares

HOT CHOCOLATE SAUCE

3 oz dark chocolate, 70% cocoa solids
½ cup heavy cream
2 teaspoons instant espresso powder dissolved in 2 tablespoons water
1 tablespoon golden syrup

1 Break up the chocolate and put into a heavy-based saucepan.

2 Add the remaining ingredients, then place the pan over a gentle heat and let everything melt together.

3 Once everything has melted, stir well, take off the heat, and pour into a jug to serve.

Makes enough to drizzle over 16 brownie squares

BLACKBERRY CRISP

Another glorious nursery-reworking, and none the worse for that. I feel that in the interests of fair trading, I should probably name this Blackberry Soggy, since what is so delish about it is its butter-fudgy topping, but since "crisp" is what these kinds of non-crumble pies are known as, I stick to that.

It's simplicity itself to make, and the daughter of a friend of mine, who had never, ever made a dessert or baked anything before, has had a runaway success with it that threatens to go, delightfully, to her head. But a dessert this good quite reasonably causes evangelical fervor. Its ease of assembly is a bonus.

To keep the costs down, you could substitute half the blackberries with chopped pears, but anyway regard this as an open blueprint and use any fruit you feel like or is on hand.

$^1/_2$ cup (1 stick) plus 1 tablespoon
   butter
$^3/_4$ cup rolled oats
$^1/_2$ cup flour
$^1/_2$ cup light brown sugar
$^1/_2$ cup flaked almonds

$^1/_4$ cup sunflower kernels
1 teaspoon ground cinnamon
4 cups blackberries
$^1/_4$ cup vanilla or granulated sugar
2 teaspoons cornstarch

1 Preheat the oven to 400°F. Melt the butter and put to one side for a mo.

2 Combine the oats, flour, brown sugar, almonds, kernels, and cinnamon in a bowl.

3 Tip the blackberries into a wide shallow baking dish (I used one here with a 3-cup capacity), sprinkle over the vanilla sugar and cornstarch, and tumble about to mix.

4 Stir the melted butter into the crisp topping and spoon on top of the blackberries to cover but not absolutely thoroughly.

5 Bake for 25 minutes and serve with ice cream or heavy cream.

Serves 4–6

CHOCOLATE MINT COOKIES

This is my version of after-dinner mints: Dispense with *dessert* and bring out a plate of minty-breathed chocolate cookies with coffee and *tisanes* instead.

These don't take long to make up and bake, and I can't tell you how lovely it is to be able to open the door to people with the smell of their baking oozing welcomingly out in the evening air.

WORKDAY WINNERS

$3/4$ cup light brown sugar	1 cup flour
$1/2$ cup (1 stick) soft butter	$1/3$ cup cocoa
1 egg	$1/2$ teaspoon baking powder
1 teaspoon vanilla extract	1 cup bittersweet chocolate chips

GLAZE:

$1/2$ cup powdered sugar	1 tablespoon unsweetened cocoa, sifted
2 tablespoons boiling water	$1/4$ teaspoon peppermint flavoring

1 Preheat the oven to 350°F.

2 Cream the sugar and butter (I use a freestanding mixer for ease), then beat in the egg and vanilla.

3 Mix the flour, cocoa, and baking powder in a bowl, and gradually beat into the creamed mixture. Finally, fold in the chips.

4 Using a rounded tablespoon measure, spoon out scoops of cookie dough and place on baking sheets lined with baking parchment or Silpat, leaving a little space in between each one.

5 Bake for 12 minutes and then let them sit on the baking sheet for a couple of minutes before moving them to a cooling rack, with some newspaper on the surface underneath.

6 Put the glaze ingredients into a saucepan and heat until combined together. Let cool completely before using.

7 Using a teaspoon, zigzag the glaze over each cooling cookie.

Makes 24

Escoffier famously said that *la nostalgie*, or homesickness, was simply a longing for the food of one's childhood. As a Frenchman living in London, he had reason to be mournful perhaps, but those of us who live in the food-fashion-obsessed world have cause for wistfulness even if we haven't transplanted ourselves. So much of what we ate when young, or what our parents and grandparents ate when young, has disappeared.

I am not sure quite whether we shun the food of our past as irrelevant and outmoded because we are less rooted in our culinary traditions than the Continental Europeans, or because, having absorbed a sense of our gastro-inferiority and desperate to show our new coolth, we are too afflicted with gawky irony. I suspect both conditions are linked. It is frankly inconceivable that anyone in France would feel that *celeriac rémoulade* were embarrassingly antique or an Italian disdain spaghetti alla carbonara for being old-fashioned. The French, the Italians love their food precisely because it's old-fashioned, because it *is* the food their grandparents ate, and they know their grandchildren will.

In other words, there is no such thing, to the cook or the eater, as Retro. And yet here I am, lamenting our shortcomings while almost boasting that I, too, possess them by virtue — vice? — of this very chapter. So be it. There are too many reasons for our being as we are to be able to disentangle or disinter now. Besides, *I* know what I mean by Retro, and I know you do, too.

Just as I think it's possible to feel an inherited nostalgia for the music one's parents listened to, so I concur that many of the recipes here more properly belong to the era of an earlier generation than mine. I love the idea — and am mad about the taste — of Crepes Suzette and Pineapple Upside-down Cake, for example, but I was scarcely brought up on them. Even worse, I feel that I am nostalgic for a period of nostalgia. All the cocktails I drank in the eighties were themselves a throwback, and self-consciously so: It was Art Deco only without the elegance. Yes, I did possess some black martini glasses — and yes, I have bought some recently, all the better to fill with White Lady (one part lemon juice to two parts Cointreau and four parts gin) and if that sounds like a camp folly, I should declare that it only *looks* like a joke.

And I suppose that's the thing: The affectation of amusement, the attitude of whimsical irony, they are just surface silliness. The real thing is, that the food we remember, or remember our parents remembering, is food we want to eat. There isn't one recipe that follows here that I don't relish and purely on gustatory terms. For what I lack in sentimentality, I more than make up for in greed.

AVOCADO CRAYFISH COCKTAIL

I eat an enormous amount of avocados. Some people are repelled by their soft-clay rich-ness; I am drawn to it. And I remember, too, when I was really quite young, just in my teens, reading that the dogs that lived in avocado orchards always had shiny, glossy coats because of all the windfall fruit they snaffled up daily. That image has stuck with me, and it is such an appealing one. I always have it in mind as I prepare myself an avocado, which is often.

And when, the other day, I found myself buying a pair of old-fashioned avocado dishes, I knew I had to be a little more backward-looking in my style of eating (most often, I just sprinkle with coarse salt and spritz with lime), so this is my version on the avocado shrimp cocktail of yore. For me, it's the way forward.

1 tomato
2 teaspoons sherry vinegar
1 teaspoon extra virgin olive oil
$^1/_2$ teaspoon kosher salt or $^1/_4$
    teaspoon table salt

$^1/_2$ cup cooked, peeled crayfish tails
1 ripe avocado
1 teaspoon chopped fresh cilantro

1 Halve the tomato, scoop out and discard the seeds, and chop what's left well, dropping the pieces into a bowl with the sherry vinegar, olive oil, and salt. Whisk to make a dressing.

2 Just before you want to eat, stir the crayfish tails into the dressing.

3 Halve the avocado, remove the pit, spoon the crayfish-tomato mixture moundingly into the hollows where the pit went, and sprinkle with the cilantro.

Serves 2

SMOKED TROUT PÂTÉ

Smoked fish was an absolute staple of my childhood — I used to have smoked mackerel with horseradish in my lunchbox — and I feel if I've got some form of smoked fish in the fridge, there is always going to be, instantly, something to eat. Pepper and lemon, that's all you need for it. And it's a gift to the cook in a hurry, too: This pâté takes the merest moment to make and yet it is a wonderful start to a meal or, indeed, a whole meal in itself. I don't even need a salad with it: I'm happy with toast, crusty bread, or maybe even some good bought English muffins or cheese scones, along with a few cornichons and any other tangy pickle.

This doesn't make very much, but it's filling and also — which is obviously how I like it — full of pep. If you want something a little milder, with less boisterous heat, then add a mere sprinkle of cayenne.

2 smoked trout fillets, about 4 oz total	2 tablespoons olive oil
1/4 cup cream cheese	1 tablespoon horseradish sauce
2 tablespoons lemon juice	1/4 teaspoon cayenne pepper

1 Put all of the above ingredients into a blender or food processor and blitz until smooth and pâté-like.

2 Spatch into a bowl — I use a small terra-cotta dish of about 4¹/₂ inches diameter — and cover with plastic wrap before chilling in the fridge.

Serves 4 as a starter

CHEF'S SALAD

I am no chef — and don't need anyone else to point that out — so perhaps this should more correctly be called Cook's Salad. Either way, it is an irresistible mix, and one that tastes so much better in the mouth than it reads on the page.

I am unapologetic about celebrating the much-maligned iceberg lettuce, and feel perfectly equable about your using the ready-torn bits of lettuce in bags. I should own up that I keep a package of ready-grated Emmental in the fridge, which I generally use in this. And there is something about canned sweet corn that is instantly comforting, especially with the cool, soft chunks of avocado. It is, indeed, the glorious mix of textures that makes this salad such a knockout. How could it ever have fallen from favor?

1 head iceberg lettuce
2 cups cubed ham ($1/2$-inch cubes)
1 cup drained canned sweet corn

1 cup grated Emmental cheese
1 ripe avocado, peeled, pitted, and
   diced

FOR THE DRESSING:
$1/2$ teaspoon Dijon mustard
1 tablespoon cabernet sauvignon
   vinegar

$1/2$ teaspoon kosher salt or $1/4$
   teaspoon table salt
3 tablespoons extra virgin olive oil

1 Tear the iceberg lettuce into pieces into a large bowl.

2 Toss in the ham, drained sweet corn, grated Emmental, and avocado chunks.

3 Whisk together the dressing ingredients in a separate bowl, and then pour over the salad before tossing everything together.

Serves 6 as a starter or 2–4 as a supper or lunch dish

Ouefs en Cocotte

My mother used to bake eggs for Sunday supper, most weeks, when I was a child — and I haven't eaten them since. Or that was until recently, when I felt an urgent and greedy need to resurrect them. My mother used to cook them in a pretty low oven for 19 minutes, and 19 minutes exactly; since this is "express," I bake mine in a moderate oven for a quarter of an hour — and lusciously perfect they are too.

The only other change I have made is an extravagant addition: I add a drop or two of white truffle oil on top of the cream, on top of the egg. Other flavor additions — a little chopped ham, diced cooked mushrooms, herbs, some sliced artichoke heart — should go in the base, before you crack in the egg.

This is a very comforting and yet luxurious starter, which helps you somewhat, in that you could give people this followed by some plain chicken and a green salad and they would consider they had feasted like oligarchs.

I am happy to spoon the creamy egg straight out of its ramekin dish but some thick slabs of toasted sourdough or good wheat bread, sliced into chunky fingers, are de rigueur as a tableside accompaniment. If you feel like pushing the boat out, consider supplying steamed asparagus spears too.

Butter for greasing
6 fabulous organic eggs
1^1/$_2$ tablespoons kosher salt

6 tablespoons heavy cream
1^1/$_2$ tablespoons white truffle oil

1 Preheat the oven to 375°F and put a full kettle of water on.

2 Dip a pastry brush in a soft stick of butter and grease 6 ramekins of about ^{1}/$_2$ cup (4 oz) capacity each, putting them into an ovenproof pan or dish as you go.

3 Crack an egg into each ramekin, followed by ^{1}/$_4$ teaspoon salt, 1 tablespoon of cream, and finally ^{1}/$_4$ teaspoon of the white truffle oil.

4 Pour boiling water into the pan to come about halfway up on each ramekin, put in the oven, and bake for 15 minutes. Serve immediately.

Serves 6

Mouclade

For some reason, this lesser-known cousin of moules mariniere has fallen from favor. That's to say, I haven't seen it on a menu or eaten it anywhere outside of my kitchen for a long time. And yet it's so good, with its creamy, mildly curried sauce.

This is very much a quick version: I use ready-washed, debearded mussels; I use scallions in place of chopped onion or shallot; and I don't sieve, strain, reduce, or any of that. It means that this is slightly soupier than the traditional version, but all the better for that. Buy a baguette or two to mop up the fragrant, creamy juices and consider yourself among the truly blessed.

4^1/$_2$ lbs mussels
4 baby leeks or scallions, finely
    sliced
2 cloves garlic, peeled and finely
    sliced

2 cups white wine or 1 cup Noilly
    Prat and 1 cup water
2 teaspoons medium Madras curry
    powder
^{1}/$_2$ cup heavy cream

1   Soak the mussels in some clean, cold water and — if they haven't been dealt with in the store — then sort through them, debearding and knocking off any barnacles with the back of a small knife.

2   Using a large pan with a lid, put in the sliced baby leeks or scallions, garlic, white wine (or Noilly Prat and water), and curry powder and bring to a boil.

3   Tip the mussels into a colander and discard any that haven't closed. Tumble the rest into the pan, clamp on the lid, and cook on high heat for about 3 minutes. Shake the pan around as they are cooking.

4   When you lift the lid the mussels should have opened. Discard any that haven't. Add the cream, and then turn into a bowl to serve or take the pan straight to the table. Remember to put out plates for the shells.

Serves 4

CHICKEN LIVER SALAD

Now this is a real blast from the past for me. I started moonlighting as a restaurant critic during the great Gastronomic Renaissance, as everyone seemed to herald it, about twenty years ago when I was an eager young thing, or almost, and there was scarcely a restaurant that didn't have a *salade tiède* of this sort on its menu. Generally, the dressing was made with raspberry vinegar, that was entirely the vogue, and I have tried to pay *homage* to this by echoing the sour-sweetness by deglazing the pan of chicken livers with maple syrup and sherry vinegar. OK, I know it sounds odd — rebarbative even — but it is a gorgeous pairing: only fugitively sweet but intense and smoky.

It also happens to be a very quick supper for two, and not the sort of quickly got-together meal that feels drearily the same.

2 tablespoons olive oil
10 oz chicken livers
8 cups arugula
1 tablespoon sherry vinegar

1 tablespoon maple syrup
1 teaspoon kosher salt or $^1/_2$ teaspoon table salt

1 Heat the oil in a heavy-bottomed skillet and cook the livers for about 7 minutes, turning the livers about in the pan regularly and squishing them as you do so to help them cook evenly.

2 While they are cooking, arrange the salad on two plates.

3 Once the livers are cooked, their rawness inside turned to moussey pink, take the pan off the heat and quickly add the vinegar and syrup to the pan.

4 Stir everything about, then divide the dressed livers between the plates with the juice from the pan.

5 Sprinkle the salt over and serve warm.

Serves 2

CHEESE FONDUE

I don't suppose this is ever going to win plaudits from the World Health Organization, but a cheese fondue is surely the stuff of dreams. On the plus side, healthwise, I love it best with radishes, endive, spears of radicchio and carrots dipped in, but I don't know why I am trying to engage with that particular argument. The point is, it makes a fabulous supper: filling, gorgeous to eat, and conducive to good atmosphere and even better spirits.

Make a vat of this, and supply nothing other than fruit afterward or, at most, a little palate-tickling sorbet.

$1^1/_4$ lbs chopped or grated cheese —
    use a mixture such as Gruyère,
    Emmental, Brie, and Camembert
$1^1/_4$ cups white wine
2 teaspoons cornstarch

3 tablespoons Kirsch
1 clove garlic, peeled
good grinding of pepper
good grating of nutmeg

TO SERVE WITH: carrot batons, trimmed radishes, radicchio, and endive cut into spears or skinny wedges, cubes of toasted sourdough, and whatever else you wish to dip

1 Put the chopped or grated cheese into the fondue pot with the wine and heat until boiling on the stove, by which time the cheese should have melted.

2 Turn the pot down to a simmer. Slake (whisk together) the cornstarch with the Kirsch in a small bowl, and add to the fondue pot along with the garlic clove.

3 Season with the pepper and nutmeg and move the fondue pot onto a flame at the table.

Serves 4

GOUJONS OF SOLE WITH DILL MAYONNAISE

Goujons have fallen out of favor over the last two decades, but it is hard to work out why. The crunch of the bread crumb casing, the tender, yielding softness of the white fish within: this is a fish finger taken to the highest level. The traditional accompaniment is tartar sauce, but my favorite is a dill mayonnaise, with perhaps some cornichons tumbled on a plate nearby.

Consider these a fabulously quick starter when you've got people over or a real treat for a midweek supper for two. The trick is to prepare ahead for that. I make up a vast batch of these and freeze them. Then, when it's dinnertime and I don't know what I'm going to cook, I heat some oil in a pan and fry a handful from frozen. They barely need an extra minute. I prefer to fry in batches in a small saucepan rather than fill a frying pan with lots of oil and try and get them all done at once.

If you can find panko, the Japanese seasoned bread crumbs, then get them: They create an almost feathery but crunchy casing.

2 lemon sole fillets, skinned	1 cup bread crumbs or 2 cups panko
$^1/_2$ cup cornstarch	1 cup peanut or grapeseed oil or as
salt and pepper	needed depending on the size of the
2 eggs	pan

1 Cut the sole fillets in half lengthwise, and then slice each fillet half into about four long strips on the diagonal. This will give you 8 goujons from each fillet.

2 Put the cornstarch into a shallow bowl and season with salt and pepper. Beat the eggs together in another bowl, and put the bread crumbs or panko into an additional shallow bowl.

3 Dip each goujon into the seasoned cornstarch, coating it well, then the beaten eggs, and finally the bread crumbs.

4 Lay the goujons on a cooling rack for a while, and heat the oil in a pan. (Or at this point you can freeze them between layers of baking parchment in an airtight container.)

5 Fry the goujons for about 2 minutes, or until crisp and golden. Remove to pieces of paper towel as you go to remove excess oil.

Makes 16, enough for about 3 people as a main course, 5 as a starter

DILL MAYONNAISE
1 cup mayonnaise, preferably organic
$^1/_3$ cup fresh dill
$^1/_2$–1 teaspoon lime juice, to taste

1 Put the mayonnaise into a bowl, and finely chop the dill, adding it to the mayo.

2 Stir in some lime juice and taste for seasoning.

CREPES SUZETTE

This is probably the queen of Retro desserts and deservedly so. This, my version, is a speeded-up and simplified one by virtue of using store-bought crepes. But there is no need to feel this is a cop-out. For one, they can be incredibly good but, more pertinently, by the time they've been doused and soused, not to mention flamed, the idea that you could discern their origins is laughable.

If you have only ever thought of crepes suzette as some amusing vestige from an irrelevant culinary canon, think again. No, just forget thought and cut straight to cooking this.

juice of 2 oranges
zest of 1 orange
$^3/_4$ cup ($1^1/_2$ sticks) butter
$^1/_3$ cup sugar

8–12 crepes
$^1/_3$ cup Grand Marnier, Cointreau, or
   triple sec

1 Pour the orange juice into a saucepan, and add the zest, butter and sugar. Bring to a boil, and then turn the heat down to a simmer, cooking for a further 10–15 minutes until the sauce becomes syrupy.

2 Fold the crepes into quarters and then arrange them in a large pan, or any flameproof dish, slightly overlapping in a circular pattern.

3 Pour over the warm syrup and then gently heat the crepes through for about 3 minutes over low heat.

4 Warm the orange liqueur of your choice in the emptied but still syrupy saucepan. When the crepes are hot in the orange sauce, pour over the liqueur and set light to the pan to flambé them. Serve immediately, spooning crepes and sauce onto each plate.

Serves 4–6

MANGO SPLIT

Even by the time I was young, a banana split had begun to lose its glory, but the notion, fruit combined with ice cream and sauce, is a good one.

I take advantage of what the Covent Garden traders used to refer to as "queer gear," i.e. exotic fruit, and replace the world's favorite fruit — bananas — with cubed mango. Rather lazily, I often buy the mangoes that my greengrocer, and all supermarkets, chop for you.

Incidentally, this is one of my children's favorite desserts, though I leave out the rum and coconut for them. For me, both resolutely stay in. I am of the More Is More school in this regard.

2 tablespoons shredded coconut	1 ripe mango or 1 tub cubed ripe
$1/4$ cup packed light brown sugar	mango
1 tablespoon butter	2 scoops vanilla ice cream
1 tablespoon lime juice	2 scoops mango sorbet
1 tablespoon dark rum	2 cigar cookies or fan wafers, optional
1 piece candied ginger, optional	

1 Toast the coconut in a dry smallish skillet until dark golden. Transfer to a small bowl to cool.

2 In a saucepan, melt the sugar, butter, lime juice, and rum and let it come to a boil and bubble for 2 minutes. Turn off the heat but leave on the stove.

3 Finely chop the candied ginger (if using) and peel, then dice the mango into about $1/2$-inch cubes.

4 Place a scoop each of vanilla ice cream and mango sorbet into 2 dessert bowls or into 2 sundae glasses.

5 Tumble in the mango cubes, then the sticky chopped ginger into each dish, and finally sprinkle over the aromatically toasted coconut.

6 Spoon over the still-warm syrup; there isn't a huge amount per dish but you don't want it swamped.

7 If the mood takes you, stick a cigar cookie or fan wafer into each sundae.

Serves 2

CHERRY CHEESECAKE

This recipe has overturned a lifetime's prejudice — which is good, but unsettling. I had always been a committed believer that the only true cheesecake was the proper, baked cheesecake, but now I'm not so sure. This improper, unbaked cheesecake, a feature on many a 1970s dessert cart, has entirely won me over. It's light, it has tang, it is rapturously good. The fact that it is speedily easy to make is more reason for general hilarity and joy.

Even in the spirit of Retro-accuracy, please do not be tempted to open a jar of cherry pie filling over the cake. I use some French cherry concoction that seems to be pretty universally available and has no added sugar, but anything labeled "conserve" as opposed to "jam" should be safe.

And, if you feel like it, when cherries are in season, strew the top with a couple of handfuls of beautiful fruit.

$1^1/_4$ cups graham cracker crumbs
6 tablespoons soft butter
2 tablespoons granualted sugar
10 oz cream cheese
$^1/_2$ cup powdered sugar
1 teaspoon vanilla extract

$^1/_2$ teaspoon lemon juice
1 cup heavy cream
1 10-oz jar **St. Dalfour Rhapsodie de Fruits Black Cherry Spread** or cherry conserve

1 Mix the graham cracker crumbs with the butter and sugar until the mixture coheres.

2 Press this mixture into an 8-inch springform pan; press a little up the sides to form a slight ridge.

3 Beat together the cream cheese, sugar, vanilla, and lemon juice in a bowl until smooth.

4 Lightly whip the cream, and then fold it into the cream cheese mixture.

5 Spoon the cheesecake filling on top of the graham cracker base and smooth with a spatula. Put it in the fridge for 3 hours or overnight.

6 When you are ready to serve the cheesecake, unmold it by removing the sides of the springform pan and spread the black cherries over the top.

Serves 6–8

PINEAPPLE UPSIDE-DOWN CAKE

This is a bit before my time, but I have vague nursery memories of a friend of my grand-mother's making a version of this, which she would serve with a warm sauce made of pineapple juice thickened with — I imagine — cornstarch. That I can do without, but I am still of the mind that it is perfectly all right to make this with canned pineapple rings. I feel it is slightly bad sport to start peeling and slicing your own pineapple.

Anyway, the canned pineapple is just fine, though I advise going for the one in its own juice rather than in syrup, and I add some of the juice to the cake batter, too. This seems to help make it light and fluffy.

I have found that the best way of keeping this swift is to bake it in my copper tarte tatin tin; if you are using a regular cake pan, be prepared to add a few minutes onto the cooking time.

Butter for greasing the pan	$^1/_2$ cup sugar
2 tablespoons sugar	2 eggs
6 slices canned pineapple rings	1 teaspoon baking powder
$^1/_3$ cup candied cherries	$^1/_4$ teaspoon baking soda
$^2/_3$ cup flour	3 tablespoons pineapple juice from
$^1/_2$ cup (1 stick) soft butter	the can of pineapple slices

1 Preheat the oven to 400°F. Butter a tarte tatin tin that is 9 inches wide at the top and 8 inches in diameter at the bottom. Or butter a cast-iron skillet or an 8- or 9-inch non-springform cake pan.

2 Sprinkle the 2 tablespoons of sugar over the buttered base, and then arrange the pine-apple slices to make a circular pattern as in the picture.

3 Fill each pineapple ring with a candied cherry, and then dot one in each of the spaces in between the rings.

4 Put the flour, butter, sugar, eggs, baking powder, and baking soda into a food processor and run the motor until the batter is smooth. Then pour in the 3 tablespoons of juice to thin it a little.

5 Pour this mixture carefully over the cherry-studded pineapple rings; it will only just cover it, so spread it out gently.

6 Bake for 30 minutes, then ease a spatula around the edge of the pan, place a plate on top, and with one deft — ha! — move, turn it upside down.

Serves 8

I don't wish to sound unsympathetic. Obviously, the fact that I am writing a book expressly concerned, as it were, with good food that can be pulled together quickly, establishes, I hope, my bona fides in this regard, but I have to own up to some degree of impatience. The thing is, whenever people, perhaps showing a slightly patronizing amusement at how often I cook (and maybe it's that which irks), claim that they themselves never have the time to cook, it makes me feel uncharacteristically aggressive. What I want to point out is that they are hardly using the time they save by *not* cooking writing *War and Peace*. I don't say that finding time to cook makes you a better person, but nor do I think that being "too busy" to cook means that your life has automatically higher purpose. And I say that as one who often professes to be beyond busy but somehow finds time to slump in front of the TV watching *CSI* repeats for hours on end.

The times I do have ready sympathy with the too frazzled and fraught to cook brigade is after children's birthday parties and at breakfast. I am not good at breakfast. I eat it because I know I must, but given a choice I would rather wait until later on in the day. Besides, since I must have two cups of tea before I even come to, it often doesn't leave a lot of time for fiddling around with breakfast, especially if your morning involves, as mine does, taking children to school.

The way of coping, I have found, is to be rather unimaginative about what you eat on waking. Just as I never got to work on time in the long-gone days when I had an office job without laying out the morning's clothes before I went to bed at night, so I find I can speed through my tasks a little faster in the morning if I know in advance what I'm going to eat for breakfast. One moment's hesitation and I become a victim of choice, overindulged and petulant and unable to be pleased.

What this means in effect is that I have month- or six-week-long runs of any given breakfast — soft-boiled egg with toast, oatmeal with blueberries, muesli with yogurt and pomegranate seeds to cite recent examples — before sliding on to the next rotation. I think, for weekdays, this makes perfect sense. But on weekends or when we're not at work, it can feel liberating to live beyond the routine.

I'm also happier on weekends to eat lunch later and therefore want a bigger breakfast, an hour or so after I've tea'd myself into consciousness. That's not to say all the recipes that follow couldn't be done during the week — they could, and easily. So please. Over to you.

Go Get 'Em Smoothie

This is truly a weekday special: a breakfast that combines food and drink for people who don't feel they've even got time to sit down in the morning.

If the person-in-a-hurry is miniature in stature, and not progressed to caffeine intake, then replace the espresso powder with a tablespoonful of peanut butter. Extra protein and ultradelicious.

I keep overripe bananas, peeled and cut into quarters, in bags in the freezer which help give ice-creamy bulk to the smoothie and dispense with the need for ice.

1 peeled frozen banana, quartered
$^2/_3$ cup milk
1 tablespoon honey
4 teaspoons chocolate malted drink powder
$^1/_2$ teaspoon instant espresso powder

1 Put all ingredients into a blender and whiz to mix.

2 Pour into a tall glass and drink before dashing out the door.

Serves 1

CHOPPED FRUIT SALAD

This is my idea of an invigorating weekday breakfast, and I make an already easy recipe even more manageable by chopping up the fruit the evening before and leaving it in covered bowls in the fridge. I know that some people might worry about the lessening of vitamin content thereby, but I assure you that unless you grow your own fruit or get up bright and early and buy it from a farmer who's just picked his, then you might as well not start worrying about how many vitamins you're losing by doing a little bit of in-advance chopping. Better than not eating at all, to be frank, and I also rather like the swallowing without chewing aspect that a little steeping gives.

This is the fruit I tend to use, although the key point here is really what I have in the fridge. The pomegranate juice below is out of a bottle, but if you're using out-of-season strawberries, use a squeeze of real juice to steep the berries and replace the mixed seeds with a gloriously jeweled topping of pomegranate instead.

1 cup finely chopped strawberries
1 teaspoon pomegranate juice
$^1/_2$ cup diced mango
$^1/_2$ teaspoon lime juice

$^3/_4$ cup blueberries
$^1/_2$ cup vanilla yogurt
2 teaspoons mixed seeds (pumpkin, sunflower, sesame)

1 Mix the chopped strawberries with the pomegranate juice.

2 Spritz the mango cubes with the lime juice.

3 Using 2 tumblers or glasses, layer the ingredients starting with the strawberries and then the mango, blueberries, yogurt, and finally the seeds.

Serves 2

BREAKFAST BRUSCHETTA

Something that is served from California to Tuscany as an evening savory or appetizer may not seem an obvious choice for breakfast, but I say: Think again. This is quick to make, absurdly easy in fact. The strange thing is that it is as easy to eat, even first thing. I can wolf this stuff down.

FOR TOMATO BRUSCHETTA:
2 tablespoons olive oil
2 thickly sliced short pieces
   sourdough toast
1 ripe tomato — approximately
   4 oz — roughly chopped
salt and pepper to taste

FOR AVOCADO BRUSCHETTA:
1 ripe avocado
2 teaspoons lime juice
salt and pepper to taste
4 thickly sliced short pieces sourdough
   toast
1 tablespoon freshly chopped parsley

1 Drizzle most of the olive oil over the toast, top with the chopped tomatoes, and season before drizzling the remaining few drops of oil on top.

2 Halve the avocado, scoop the flesh into a bowl, and mash roughly using a fork along with the lime juice. Season to taste.

3 Spread clumpingly on each waiting piece of toast and sprinkle with the parsley.

Serves 3 to 6, depending on appetite

HOMEMADE INSTANT PANCAKE MIX

This is going to change your life irrevocably. Forgive any scintilla of self-congratulatory preening and accept my boast as simple, enthusiastic exuberance. That is the spirit in which it is intended. But I tell you: Just mix the ingredients, keep them in a container at easy reach, and then every time you are required to be the usher-forth of good things of a morning, just scoop some dry mixture out, mix and whisk together with egg, milk, and melted butter, by hand or in a blender — and that's it. Pancakes aplenty, without even having to think about it. You know it makes sense.

FOR THE PANCAKE MIX:

4 cups flour

3 tablespoons baking powder

2 teaspoons baking soda

1 teaspoon salt

2 tablespoons plus 2 teaspoons sugar

Mix the above ingredients together and store in a jar.

TO MAKE THE BATTER AND THE PANCAKES:

To make the pancakes, for each 1 cup of pancake mix, add and whisk together:

1 egg

1 cup milk

1 tablespoon butter, melted

1 Heat a dry flat griddle or pan — no need to oil it.

2 Spoon $1^1/_2$ to 2 tablespoons of batter onto the hot griddle and when bubbles appear on the surface of the little pancakes, flip them over to make them golden brown on both sides. A minute or so a side should do it.

Makes 15 pancakes of about 3 inches in diameter

Blueberry Syrup for Pancakes

According to those who make it their business to know such things, both maple syrup and blueberries are supremely health-giving and wondrously good for you. This is fine by me, since I love them, separately and — by way of a new experiment — in combination. If you have any left over, you will notice that it sets into a kind of glossy jam. This will keep for a few days in a jar and put in the fridge, and is glorious dolloped into yogurt or spread on bread.

$^1/_2$ **cup maple syrup**

$1^1/_2$ **cups blueberries**

1 Put the syrup and blueberries into a pan and bring to a boil.

2 Let bubble for 8–10 minutes, and then pour into a pitcher and bring to the breakfast table with the pancakes.

Makes enough for the pancakes, above

Breakfast Bars

I am addicted to these, and so is everyone I give them to. Although they're quick to throw together, they do take nearly an hour to bake, so what I suggest is, make a batch on the weekend and then you will have the oaty, chewy bars ready and waiting for those days when you have to snatch breakfast on the run.

Mind you, they are just like milk and cereal in bar form, so there's nothing to stop you nibbling one with your morning coffee at home every day. If you are not a morning person, believe me, they will make your life easier.

They also store well; indeed, they seem to get better and better. So just stash them in a tin and remove when you want.

1 14-fl-oz can condensed milk
2^1/$_2$ cups rolled oats (not instant)
1 cup shredded coconut
1 cup dried cranberries

1 cup mixed seeds (pumpkin, sunflower, sesame)
1 cup natural unsalted peanuts

1   Preheat the oven to 250°F and oil a 9 x 13-inch baking pan or just use a disposable aluminium foil one.

2   Warm the condensed milk in a large pan.

3   Meanwhile, mix all the other ingredients together and add the warmed condensed milk, using a rubber spatula to fold and distribute.

4   Spread the mixture into the oiled or foil pan and press down with a spatula or, better still, your hands (wearing those disposable latex *CSI* gloves to stop you from sticking) to make the surface even.

5   Bake for 1 hour, remove, and after about 15 minutes, cut into four across and four down, to make 16 chunky bars. Let cool completely.

Makes 16

PEAR AND GINGER MUFFINS

These are particularly good: nothing fancy (I hate a breakfast muffin that thinks it's a cake), but the pear keeps the texture luscious and the ginger permeates everything, including your kitchen, with its husky heat. This makes for the kind of Saturday breakfast I can happily settle into. And I'm pretty keen on a quick snack later on in the day of one of these now cooled muffins with some sharp, hard cheese, a Cheddar maybe or Caerphilly, or a crumbly, pungent blue.

You can mix all the dry ingredients in a bowl, and the wet ones in a large measuring cup, cover both with plastic wrap, and leave the former in a cool spot in the kitchen and the latter in the fridge. Then all you have to do is peel and chop the pear and fork everything lazily together. I dare say you will not get punished from on high if you don't bother to peel the pear, either. I do, simply because I love the way the juicy fruit merges with the crumb when there are no barriers to its oozing.

1³/₄ cups flour
3/₄ cup granulated sugar
¹/₂ cup plus 6 teaspoons packed
  light brown sugar
2 teaspoons baking powder
1 teaspoon ground ginger

²/₃ cup sour cream
¹/₂ cup vegetable oil
1 tablespoon honey
2 eggs
1¹/₂ cups peeled and chopped pears,
  about ¹/₄-inch dice

1 Preheat the oven to 400°F, and line a 12-cup muffin pan with paper muffin cups.

2 Measure into a bowl the flour, granulated sugar, the ¹/₂ cup of brown sugar, baking powder, and ground ginger.

3 In a large measuring cup, whisk the sour cream, oil, honey, and eggs together and then fold this into the dry ingredients.

4 Lastly, mix in the pear dice and then divide the batter evenly among the muffin cups.

5 Sprinkle each one with ¹/₂ teaspoon brown sugar and then bake for 20 minutes. Remove to a cooling rack. Best eaten still a little warm.

Makes 12

CHOCOLATE CROISSANTS

First let me say to you that if I can do this, you can. As I have never tried to hide, I have no patience and even less dexterity. But this is child's play: Indeed, you could consider getting children to make them. They certainly like eating them, and they tend to like eating what they make themselves even more.

Half a 17.2-oz packet ready-rolled butter puff pastry
2$^1/_2$ oz chocolate (milk or dark depending on taste)
1 egg, beaten

1 Preheat the oven to 425°F. Unfurl the sheet of pastry and then cut it into 4 squares.

2 Cut each square diagonally to give 2 triangles (they will appear quite small). Put the triangle with the wider part facing you and the point away from you.

3 Break off small pieces of chocolate (approx. $^1/_2$ inch) to place about $^3/_4$ inch up from the wide end nearest you.

4 Then carefully roll from that chocolate-loaded end toward the point of the triangle.

5 You should now have something resembling a straight croissant. Seal it lightly with your fingertips and curl it around into a crescent.

6 Place the chocolate croissants on a baking sheet lined with baking parchment, aluminum foil, or Silpat and paint with the beaten egg. Bake for 15 minutes until golden and puffy and exuberantly, if miniaturely, croissant-like.

Makes 8

ORANGE FRENCH TOAST

There is not a type of French toast I don't love, but this version, a kind of eggy, squidgy toast and marmalade, is the perfect mixture between morning-sharp and weekend treatiness.

2 eggs
$^1/_4$ cup whole milk
$^1/_4$ teaspoon ground cinnamon
grated zest of 1 orange
2 large, thick slices white bread or 4 smaller slices

juice of an orange
$^1/_4$ cup fine cut orange marmalade such as Tiptree "Crystal"
$^1/_4$ cup sugar
1 tablespoon butter

1 Whisk the eggs, milk, cinnamon, and orange zest in a wide shallow dish.

2 Soak the bread slices in this mixture for 2 minutes a side.

3 While the eggy bread is soaking, bring the orange juice, marmalade, and sugar to a boil, then turn down to a fast simmer for 3–4 minutes. If you need to, let this syrup stand while you cook the bread.

4 Heat the tablespoon of butter in a skillet and cook the eggy bread for about 2 minutes a side over medium heat until golden.

5 Serve the French toast with some of the amber syrup poured over each slice, and a pitcher of extra syrup on the side.

Serves 2

GREEN EGGS AND HAM

This is another brunch dish which, frankly, can be eaten at any time of the day with equal relish and has also in its favor that children (who in my experience would probably eat anything if it had pesto in it) love it. This is entirely proper, of course, given that — very obviously — the recipe is inspired by the Good Doctor.

      What you're making in effect are pesto pancakes — and these will be better if you use "fresh" pesto that comes in a plastic tub, not in a jar — which can be whizzed up in a blender and then needs a moment or two in a hot pan before being wrapped around finely sliced, tenderly pink ham.

$^2/_3$ cup low-fat milk	1 egg
$^1/_2$ cup pesto	oil for frying
$^1/_2$ cup flour	5 large thin ham slices

1 Blend or whisk together the milk, pesto, flour, and egg to make a batter.

2 Oil a crepe pan or heavy-bottomed skillet, wiping away any excess oil with a paper towel, and place over medium heat.

3 Ladle in approximately $^1/_3$–$^1/_2$ cup of batter, swirling instantly to gain a paper-thin crepe.

4 Once the top becomes dry and the edges lift away, flick it over with a thin rubber or wooden spatula for about 30 seconds to cook the other side.

5 Layer the pancakes between pieces of baking parchment or wax paper as you go, and when you have finished making them lay a slice of ham on each one and roll into triangles or however you like!

Makes 5

FRITTATA PARTY!

I love the sort of thin omelettes the Italians sometimes turn into sandwiches: cold and pressed between two pieces of mayonnaised bun or slices of schiacciata. And that's what I'd warmly advise here in the unlikely event that you end up with leftovers. But they are so good hot and straight off the press, eaten either with knife and fork or rolled up within a warmed tortilla, that I urge you to morph into a kind of short-order omelette cook next time you have a batch of people to feed convivially in the morning or not long after.

The way to make this easy is, first get a good pan (I like a Scanpan Crepe Pan), then get out loads of eggs and leave them out near a mixing bowl by the stove, and then mix up a few ideas for fillings and set them out in their bowls nearby. Then, all you do is crack two eggs, add your filling, fry, toss out, and get on with the next.

I've jotted down what I put in the omelettes opposite. Obviously, I don't expect you to be restricted, but I thought it might be helpful.

FOR EACH OMELETTE:
2 eggs
1/2 teaspoon butter and a drop of oil
   for frying

FOR THE CHEESE OMELETTE:
1/4 cup grated Emmental (but any
   cheese should do)

FOR THE CHILE OMELETTE:
1 long red chile, deseeded and sliced
1/4 teaspoon ground coriander
1/4 teaspoon ground ginger

FOR THE GREEN OMELETTE:
1/2 cup watercress or baby spinach (or,
   indeed, arugula, finely chopped)
1 scallion, finely sliced

FOR THE HAM OMELETTE:
1/2 cup chopped ham

1 Beat the eggs with the filling of your choice.

2 Heat a crepe pan or heavy-bottomed skillet with the butter and oil.

3 Once the pan is hot, pour in the egg mixture, swirling quickly to get an even and thin coating in the pan.

4 Let the omelette cook for a couple of minutes over medium-high heat.

5 Lift the edge of the omelette with a spatula to check that it is set and golden underneath; the top of the omelette should be just about set but still a little gooey.

6 Slip the omelette out of the pan onto a plate and flip one half of the omelette over the other, or fold in 3 like a business letter. Carry on!

CROQUE MONSIEUR BAKE

Like many good brunch recipes, this is also just the ticket for an early evening supper, the sort you eat in your dressing gown before sophisticated adults feel it is entirely proper to dine.

The joy of this is that you make up the mustardy ham and Gruyère sandwiches and cover with beaten eggs the night before, and just let them sit in the fridge, melding into one savory, gooey pudding overnight. The next morning goes as follows: oven on; egg-and-bread dish in; brunch effortlessly served.

6 slices ready-sliced multigrain brown
   bread
$1/3$ cup Dijon mustard
4 oz Gruyère cheese slices
3 slices/3 oz ham
6 eggs
1 teaspoon kosher salt or $1/2$
   teaspoon table salt

$1/3$ cup whole milk
4 tablespoons grated Gruyère,
   Emmental, or Cheddar
good sprinkling of Worcestershire
   sauce

1 Spread the mustard on the bread slices and make sandwiches with the fine slices of cheese and ham. Put each slice of cheese against the mustardy bread, and the ham between them. Make the sandwich and cut each one in half, making two triangles.

2 Squish the sandwiches into a baking dish approximately $10^1/2$ by $8^1/4$ inches and $2^1/4$ inches deep.

3 Beat together the eggs, salt, and milk (I measure out the milk into whatever the mustard's been in for maximum flavor penetration) and then pour this over the sandwiches tightly packed in the dish.

4 Cover the dish with plastic wrap and leave in the fridge overnight.

5 Next morning, preheat the oven to 400°F and take the dish out of the fridge, removing the plastic wrap.

6 Sprinkle over the grated cheese and Worcestershire sauce and bake in the oven for 25 minutes.

Serves 4–6

Quick
Quick

Slow

I have never quite understood why people are so obsessed with how long a recipe takes or, rather, how long something takes to cook. Certainly, I would never suggest my slow-cooked 24-hour pork when you get home from work at seven and have people coming to eat at eight. That would be silly. But for most of our lives, the time needed to cook something is the least stressful aspect; what you should be considering is how much time you are required to spend in the kitchen. This is why I would so much rather, when I'm tired and lacking in impetus and inspiration, put a chicken in to roast — which will take an hour or so to cook, during which time I am not needed — than start chopping up things to stir-fry, which might take only ten minutes but for all of those ten minutes, I will be required to busy myself frenetically.

I exult in the liberation that comes from slow-cooking. And I adore the feeling of security and messy organization that emanates from the cozy knowledge that there is something gently braising away in the oven or, even, still snugly wrapped in the fridge, ready and waiting for its oven time. This, for me, is one of the small pleasures of every-day life. It makes me feel involved in the kitchen, with food, when I'm busy elsewhere. I can't set aside huge tracts of time to get every meal ready when it's needed, so what I do is a little bit of prep here and there, a five-minute think-about and planning, so that when I do need to cook, it's nearly all taken care of. All I have to do is apply heat.

I don't have a vigorous do-it-ahead plan of attack, but I try and take some of the steps early. So, I stash steaks and chicken parts in marinades so that I've got something ready to be flung on a grill or under a broiler without forethought at the end of the day. And the one thing I feel utterly beaten by when I'm really tired is the idea of peeling and chopping onions. I don't actually find it difficult, but the thought is a daunting one. So, when I have time to spare (usually when I'm avoiding something I should be doing), I peel, chop, and fry onions slowly and gently to a gorgeous mush that can be frozen in cubes and thawed to form the basis for a stew or sauce when needed.

I also like a small amount of quietly satisfying jar-filling in my life. It's scarcely strenuous, deeply enjoyable, and also means you have the wherewithal for dessert when-ever you want at some unforeseen future point. I fill a jar with golden sultanas and pour Grand Marnier over them and let them steep. I've also been known to go the more traditional rum'n'raisin route, and very good they both are. I put morello cherries and cherry brandy in a jar, and — a very recent innovation and rubily gorgeous — mix dried cherries and berries, that's how they're labeled, with a pomegranate liqueur called Pama. Any of these is exquisite tumbled over ice cream.

Slow-cooking, quite simply, can be the express route. When you think about it, there is almost a cosmic pathos about our contemporary belief that you can "save" time. I can save you energy and, importantly, stress.

Besides, I can't live every minute of my life as a spinning top, whipping myself to go ever faster. My quick-quick-slow approach isn't just about offering practical help; it actually changes the emotional tenor of the house.

MAPLE CHICKEN'N'RIBS

This recipe says it all. You need no more than a few minutes to load up a couple of freezer bags with ribs and chicken, oils, and unguents and then after a day or so's untroublesome marinating in the fridge, you tip out the contents to a roasting pan and slot it in the oven. Your input is minimal, but what you get is a big feast that feels homey and welcoming and makes everyone happy, you included.

12 pork spareribs	2 tablespoons vegetable oil
12 chicken thighs, skin and bone still on	2 tablespoons soy sauce
	2 star anise
1 cup apple juice, as sharp as possible	1 cinnamon stick, halved
$^1/_4$ cup maple syrup	6 unpeeled cloves garlic

1 Put the ribs and chicken pieces in a couple of large freezer bags or into a dish.

2 Add all the remaining ingredients, squelching or tossing everything together well before sealing the bags or covering the dish.

3 Leave to marinate in the fridge overnight or up to two days.

4 Take the dish out of the fridge and preheat the oven to 400°F.

5 Pour the contents of the freezer bag into 1 or 2 large roasting pans (making sure the chicken is skin side up), place in the preheated oven, and cook for about $1^1/_4$ hours, by which time everything should be sticky and glossed chestnut brown.

Serves 6–8

CRISPY DUCK

I've always thought one of the best ways to eat duck was as the Chinese do, but I had never thought it would be so easy to cook. I say "cook." I do nothing except cut some fat off the duck and sit it on a rack in a pan and put it in the oven for hours on end. Then I take it out, set to with some forks, and put some store-bought Chinese pancakes on to steam. I chop and slice cucumber and scallions and open a jar of hoisin sauce. Actually, come to think of it, I nearly always ask someone else to open it for me. This could hardly be easier. What's more, children seem to adore it, which makes it a really lovely family Saturday dinner. It's easy to add another duck if there are even more of you eating.

1 duck	$^1/_2$ cucumber
4–6 store-bought Chinese pancakes	6 scallions
10 oz jar hoisin sauce	

1 Preheat the oven to 325°F.

2 Cut off the flap of fat that hangs over the duck's cavity. Sit the trimmed duck on a rack or slotted tray over a deep roasting pan and roast for 4 hours.

3 Turn the oven up to 450°F and give a final 30 minutes of intense heat. Or, if it's easier, just leave the duck in the low oven for $5^1/_2$ hours. The choice is yours.

4 Sit the pancakes on the top part of a steamer to cook or simply follow instructions on the package. Pour the sauce in a bowl with a spoon.

5 Cut the cucumber into matchsticks (like you get in a Chinese restaurant).

6 Cut the scallions lengthways into short strips (again, like they do in Chinese restaurants).

7 Carefully take the roasting pan out of the oven and transfer the duck onto a board. When you can handle it comfortably, shred it and set it on the table with the sauce, cucumber, scallion shreds, and pancakes. Wrap the duck meat, topped with the sauce, cucumbers, and scallion, in the pancakes. When the duck fat has cooled a little, pour it into a bowl or jar. It makes great fried potatoes.

Serves 4–6

LAMB, OLIVE, AND CARAMELIZED ONION TAGINE

Nearly all stews start with chopped onions. This is the lazy person's version, which uses some sweet onion confit out of a jar instead (though if you've made some of your own onion mush, do use that). And I add to the desirable idleness by not even searing the meat. I just tip everything into a big pan and let it do its own sweet thing without any interference from me. I don't actually cook this in a tagine — though I often serve it in one — but ever since someone told me that in Morocco most tagines are made in pressure cookers, I have felt unembarrassed by calling something cooked in a pan a tagine. And by all means use a pressure cooker if you're that way inclined. I've tried them, but always return to pots and pans that don't hiss at me.

I prefer to cook this in a low oven rather than on the stove, but a licking simmer would do as well. Like all stews, it benefits by being cooked in advance, so it makes sense to cook this on a day when you've got time, and eat it — reheating it on the stove, all of it, or in batches as suits — when you're in more of a hurry.

The quickest, and most suitable, accompaniment is a bowl of couscous, pale and plain or studded with a can or two of chickpeas.

2¼ lbs diced leg of lamb
1 head of garlic, separated into cloves
12 oz pitted black olives in brine, 5 oz drained weight to give 1¼ cups
½ cup caramelized onions from a jar

4 tablespoons capers
2 teaspoons ground cumin
2 teaspoons ground ginger
1 750ml bottle red wine

1 Preheat the oven to 300°F.

2 Put all of the ingredients into a casserole or heavy-bottomed pan, pouring in the wine last and giving everything a good stir.

3 Bring the pan to a boil, then clamp on the lid and put into the oven for 2 hours or until the lamb is very tender.

Serves 6–8

LAMB SHANKS WITH BEANS

The trouble with the sort of speedy cooking that can't help but be the mainstay of our daily repertoire is that it necessarily leaves out the food that makes you feel cozy rather than briskly efficient. But even if I know I've only got ten minutes of free time over two days, I can still make sure I get something big and bolstering on the table. On one day I stick my lamb shanks in to marinate, on the other I put them in the oven, leaving them there while I battle over homework or try and clear my desk or whatever other doomed task I set myself.

The beans I'm happy to get out of a can. I love their pinks and browns and tones of Tuscan stone and they turn a pile of bones into a feast.

1 cup white wine	6 lamb shanks
4 tablespoons red currant jelly plus 1 teaspoon	$^1/_4$ cup water
2 tablespoons Worcestershire sauce	1 tablespoon Dijon mustard
$^1/_4$ cup garlic-infused oil plus 2 tablespoons	4 14-oz cans mixed beans (sometimes sold as mixed bean salad)
2 onions, quartered	salt and pepper to taste
3-inch sprig rosemary or 1 teaspoon dried	

1 Get out two freezer bags and divide the wine, all but the 1 teaspoon of red currant jelly, Worcestershire sauce, the garlic oil, and rosemary between them. Add the shanks, 3 to a bag. Seal and put in the fridge overnight or up to 2 days.

2 When the shanks have had their marinating time, take them out of the fridge and preheat the oven to 425°F.

3 Tip the contents of the bags into a foil-lined roasting pan and slot this in the oven, turning it down immediately to 325°F and roast for 1$^1/_2$ hours, then remove the shanks to a warmed dish.

4 In a pan big enough to hold the beans, warm the water, remaining 2 tablespoons of garlic oil, teaspoon of red currant jelly, and the Dijon mustard. Stir to combine and add the beans, heating them gently and stirring occasionally with a wooden spoon. Season to taste and then add to the dish with the shanks. Serve with more red currant jelly and perhaps a tomato salad alongside.

Serves 6

Coq au Riesling

I have always loved the Alsatian version of coq au vin and this is it, stunningly streamlined. I replace the onion with leek, buy bacon already cubed, and buy chicken thighs. The dark meat is always best in a stew. I don't bother to sear the meat, which really means you need skinless portions; unbrowned chicken skin is not pretty. If you're not buying thighs, but thigh fillets, then it is probably more helpful to think in terms of boned weight, rather than number of portions: go, here, for about 2 3/4 pounds.

I tend not to add any cream to this the first time around, which is why I mention it in the ingredients list but not in my method, but if I have a small amount left over, I add a little heavy cream and turn it into a pasta sauce. I like to eat my coq au Riesling as they do in Alsace, with a huge pile of buttered noodles. Whether you add cream or not is entirely up to you.

2 tablespoons garlic-infused oil	10 oz oyster mushrooms, torn into
1 cup cubed bacon	strips (4 cups)
1 leek, finely sliced	3 bay leaves
12 skinless chicken thighs or 2 3/4	salt and pepper to taste
pounds thigh fillets	heavy cream, optional
1 750-ml bottle Riesling wine	1 to 2 tablespoons freshly chopped dill

1 Heat the oil in a casserole or large wide pan and fry the bacon until crisp.

2 Add the sliced leek and soften it with the bacon for a minute or so.

3 Tip in the chicken thighs, wine, mushrooms, and bay leaves.

4 Season with salt and pepper and bring to a boil, cover the pan, and simmer gently for 30–40 minutes, stirring in the cream for the last couple of minutes if you want. Like all stews, this tastes its mellowest best if you let it get cold and then reheat the next day. But it's no hardship to eat straight off. Whichever, serve sprinkled with dill, and with some buttered noodles on the side.

Serves 6

SWEDISH SALMON

I think of this as a curious amalgam of my two grandmothers. My maternal grand-mother was a passionate, if that is the right word to describe stirrings for the frozen north, espouser of all things Swedish — design, decor, dill. My paternal grandmother taught me to cook salmon this way, and there is no better. That's to say, you don't really cook it, you just get it hot and let it get cold. I promise you, you have never tasted cold poached salmon till you have tasted it this way: Its tender coral flesh is delicate but fla-vorsome and it makes cooking for a big crowd — think weekend lunch in the summer — almost disconcertingly easy.

For me it has to be eaten with the mustardy dill sauce, which is why I have merged the two recipes (though feel free to substitute a plate of lemon or lime wedges, but either way, sit the salmon on a plate lined with watercress or other peppery leaves) and, for choice, with the cucumber and potato salads that follow.

If it makes you feel more positive, believe me you don't have to have any expe-rience filleting fish. I find that cooked like this, you can just lift up the tail end and start slicing and the whole top fillet will come off in your hands; remove the backbone and you have the other. But sometimes I just cut off pieces, as anyway, I think they look better on the plate if not in huge chunks. There are too many variables at play to be precise about how long the salmon will take to cook, but if you're planning to eat it for supper, make it in the morning; if you want it for lunch, then prepare it the previous day or evening.

1 salmon — preferably wild — approx. 5 lbs, cleaned and scaled	2 tablespoons granulated sugar
1 oz fresh dill plus 3 tablespoons chopped dill	1 teaspoon peppercorns
4 whole scallions	3 tablespoons Dijon mustard
2 tablespoons plus 1 teaspoon kosher salt, or 1 tablespoon plus $1/2$ teaspoon table salt	2 tablespoons light brown sugar
	1 cup sour cream
	3 tablespoons white wine vinegar

1 Lay the salmon in a roasting pan, cutting its head and/or tail off if necessary, and stuff the cavity with the bunch of dill.

2 Add the scallions, 2 tablespoons of salt, the granulated sugar, and the peppercorns. Pour in enough cold water so that the salmon is just covered.

3 Put on the heat and bring to a boil, turn down to a gentle simmer, cover with aluminum foil, and let bubble timidly for 10 minutes.

4 Remove the pan from the stove and turn the salmon over. Don't worry about ripping the skin as you will be filleting it later. Let it cool, covered loosely with baking parchment or wax paper.

5 When the water's cold, the salmon will be perfectly cooked and very, very succulent and tender.

6 Remove the salmon from its cold poaching liquid to a large piece of wax paper or baking parchment. Remove the skin, and carefully cut fillets off the fish in whatever way is easiest for you.

7 Arrange on a serving plate and get on with the sauce.

8 Whisk together the mustard and brown sugar and when mixed, whisk in the sour cream and vinegar. Season to taste with salt. Whisk in the chopped dill. Transfer to a pitcher to serve alongside the salmon.

Serves 10–12

Sweet and Sour Cucumber Salad

I love this Middle European summer salad. It is also unfathomably good with hot frankfurters. Even though it does get a little waterier, it is still fantastic after it's been sitting in the fridge for a while, which makes it another easy do-ahead dish. Just transfer to a serving bowl with a spatula if need be.

2 medium cucumbers	2 teaspoons kosher salt or 1 teaspoon
2 teaspoons sugar	table salt
2 tablespoons white wine vinegar	$^1/_4$ cup finely chopped dill

1 Peel and finely slice the cucumbers into wafer-thin circles and transfer to a large bowl.

2 In a measuring cup, whisk together the sugar, vinegar, and salt and pour over the cucumbers, turning well to mix.

3 Add the chopped dill, toss again, and then turn into a shallow serving dish. Or else, cover with plastic wrap and chill in the fridge until needed (up to 4 hours).

Serves 10–12

Quick Quick Slow

Warm Potato Salad

I have a difficulty with those potato salads that are claggy with mayo and that burn the esophagus with too enthusiastic a scattering of raw onion. This is more my thing: no peeling — to start with — and then, finally, a sousing with white wine vinegar mixed with mustard and bacon. And the scallions are gentle. I love it warm, but so long as you mix the dressing and the potatoes while they're themselves warm, it doesn't matter if you eat the salad cold. Or, rather, at room temperature: Do not chill it in the fridge. And don't crumble the bacon over till you're ready to serve it.

$4^1/_2$ lbs baby new potatoes	8 slices bacon
4 scallions, finely sliced	1–2 teaspoons white wine vinegar
1 tablespoon garlic-infused oil	1 tablespoon whole-grain mustard

1 Bring a pan of salted water to a boil and tip in the potatoes. Cook for 20 minutes or until tender, then drain and cut in half (if you can be bothered).

2 Put the potatoes into a large bowl and add the scallions.

3 Heat the oil in the warm potato pan and cook the bacon until really crispy, then remove to a plate.

4 Take off the heat and add the vinegar and mustard. Give a little stir, then tip in the potatoes and scallions and toss everything together before transferring to a serving bowl. You can leave it like this for an hour or so.

5 When you are ready to serve it, crumble over most of the crisp bacon and toss again, then sprinkle with the remaining bits of bacon.

Serves 10–12

GRAVLAX SASHIMI

This was not intended to be the Swedish portion of the book, but it occurred to me after making some gravlax a Christmas or so ago that the method would be a very good way of curing a piece of salmon to create fear-free sashimi at home.

Obviously, as well as having some Japanese flavors — the wasabi and sake, and no dill — this is a completely effort-free take on what can be a little fiddly.

You can buy the piece of salmon at the supermarket, along with the flavorings, and everything goes in a dish in the fridge and is just left there for three days, and up to five.

It makes a different kind of supper and a very good one: You can eat it as if it were Scandinavian, along with rye bread and gherkins, or as here, with more of a nod to its Japanese association, with sushi rice, pickled ginger, and a blob or two of wasabi.

1 lb skinless salmon fillet
3 tablespoons kosher salt
3 tablespoons sugar

$1^1/_2$ tablespoons sake
1 tablespoon wasabi

QUICK QUICK SLOW

1 Put the salmon in a glass dish.

2 Mix the salt, sugar, sake, and wasabi paste in a little bowl and smear half of it over the salmon. Turn the salmon over and smear over the rest.

3 Cover the dish with plastic wrap, making sure you press down on the salmon and in the corners before bringing it over and down the sides of the dish.

4 Place cans of vegetables or unopened jars of pickles on the salmon to weight it and put everything in the fridge for at least 2 days and up to 5.

5 When you want to eat it, remove the salmon from the dish and wipe it with paper towels. Put it on a board and cut down into strips, then cut each strip into 2 or 3 pieces to make sashimi-suitable shapes.

Serves 8

MOONBLUSH TOMATOES

I used to balk at the "sunblush" tomatoes you can get at specialty shops, the sort that are dried down to essence of tomato and steeped in oregano and oil. But I find them incredibly useful and disconcertingly good. I'd tried making my own in the past, but even when barely on, my oven seemed too hot for the job. Now, though, I've hit on the way, which is simply to put them in a very hot oven, turn it off, and leave the tomatoes overnight; hence "moon" blush. I am addicted to making them now. Feel free to substitute the homespun variety in any recipe that stipulates store-bought sunblush tomatoes and I've put one of my favorite recipes for their usage below, too. Frankly, though, they're wonderful eaten just as they are, with bread, cheese, or as a salad.

And I also make them exactly the same way with large tomatoes, roughly chopped — and see them looking glorious with the tuna on page 151. This makes a fabulous instant pasta sauce, too.

1 lb, about 24 in number, on-the-vine cherry or other baby tomatoes	2 teaspoons kosher salt
2 tablespoons olive oil	1 teaspoon dried thyme
	$1/4$ teaspoon sugar

1 Preheat the oven to 450°F.

2 Cut the tomatoes in half and sit them cut side up in an ovenproof dish. Sprinkle over the olive oil, salt, thyme, and sugar.

3 Put them in the oven and immediately turn it off. Leave the tomatoes in the oven overnight or for a day without opening it.

SLOW-ROAST TOMATOES, GOAT CHEESE, AND MINT SALAD

8–10 cups arugula or spinach leaves	2 tablespoons extra virgin olive oil
1 cup soft goat cheese, such as Chavrie	1 tablespoon lemon juice
1 batch Moonblush Tomatoes, opposite	2 tablespoons freshly chopped mint

1 Arrange the arugula or spinach on a large dish, then scoop out spoonfuls of the soft goat cheese and dollop it here and there.

2 Add the cooked-down, intensely red tomato halves.

3 In the dish the tomatoes had been cooking in, whisk together the oil and lemon juice and pour over the salad.

4 Scatter with mint.

Serves 8

LAZY LOAF

It is heartening to know that you can be in a permanent hurry and not spend more than a few minutes at any time anywhere, let alone just in the kitchen — and still make a beautiful loaf of bread.

This is it — a few ingredients lazily stirred together in a bowl, and then into a bread pan in the oven. There is no kneading or rising. It feels like a cheat, but it isn't. It's the right, real thing.

2³/₄ cups wholewheat bread flour
2 cups best-quality oaty unsugared muesli (do not use granola)
2¹/₂ teaspoons (1 package) rapid-rise or instant yeast

2 teaspoons kosher salt or 1 teaspoon table salt
1 cup 2% milk
1 cup water

1 Mix the flour, muesli, yeast, and salt in a bowl, then pour in the milk and water and stir to mix. It will be a thick porridge.

2 Transfer to a greased or silicon 2 lb loaf pan; I like one that's deep and short rather than shallow. Put this in a cold oven, turning it immediately on to 225°F, and leave at this temperature for 45 minutes.

3 When these 45 minutes are up, turn the oven temperature up to 350°F and leave for 1 hour, by which time the bread should be golden and cooked through. Slip it out of its pan and although dense — it is that kind of loaf — it should feel slightly hollow when you knock it underneath. You can always slip it back in the oven, out of its pan, for a few minutes if you think it needs more baking.

4 Remove to a rack and let cool.

No-Churn Pomegranate Ice Cream

It's not hard to think of a dessert that can be made in advance. But mostly the advantage is simply that all the effort is upfront and early. The thing about this recipe is that you do it in advance — it's ice cream, so that stands to reason — but what you do in advance is negligible in terms of effort. You don't make a custard, and you don't have to keep whipping it out of the deep freeze to beat the crystals out of it. No, you simply squeeze and stir.

On top of that cause for greater contentment, there is also the fact that this delicate pink ice cream tastes like fragrant, sherbety heaven.

2 pomegranates	1^1/$_2$ cups powdered sugar
1 lime	2 cups heavy cream

1 Juice the pomegranates and the lime, straining the juices into a bowl. You will have approximately $3/4$ cup of pomegranate juice. Reserve the pomegranate seeds for garnish.

2 Add the powdered sugar and whisk to dissolve.

3 Whisk in the cream and keep whisking until soft peaks form in the pale pink cream.

4 Spoon and smooth the ice cream into a rigid plastic container with a tight-fitting lid and freeze for at least 4 hours or overnight. Scatter with pomegranate seeds when you eat it.

Serves 8

IRISH CREAM TIRAMISU

I've long been tinkering about with a bottle of Baileys, seeing how it could best be called upon in the kitchen, and I think, with this, I've found it. An Italian friend of mine, who makes a killer tiramisu herself, was an instant convert. I was relieved; the Italians generally are conservative about their food, which goes some way to explaining the longevity of their cherished culinary traditions. But this only sounds like some sort of joke — "Did you hear the one about the Irishman and the Italian . . . ?" — and in reality is an elegantly buff-tinted, creamy-toned variant of the punchy if comfortably clichéd original.

1¹/₂ cups espresso coffee, made with 1¹/₂ cups water and 9 teaspoons instant espresso powder
1 cup Baileys Irish Cream liqueur
2 7.05-oz packages Savoiardi (Italian ladyfinger) cookies or other ladyfingers

2 eggs
¹/₃ cup sugar
1 lb/2 cups mascarpone cheese
2¹/₂ teaspoons cocoa

1 Make the coffee and let it cool (the espresso powder does mix fairly well in room temperature water).

2 Mix the coffee and 3/4 cup of the Baileys together in a shallow bowl.

3 Dip the ladyfingers into this liquid; let them soak on each side enough to become damp but not soggy. Line the bottom of an 8¹/₂-inch square glass dish with a layer of ladyfingers.

4 Separate the eggs, but keep only one of the whites. Whisk the two yolks and sugar together until thick and a paler yellow, then fold in the remaining quarter cup of Baileys and the mascarpone to make a moussey mixture.

5 Whisk the single egg white until thick and frothy; you can do this by hand with such a little amount. Fold the egg white into the yolky mascarpone, and then spread half of this mixture on top of the layer of ladyfingers.

6 Repeat with another layer of soaked ladyfingers, and then top with the remaining mascarpone mixture.

7 Cover the dish with plastic wrap and leave in the fridge overnight. When you are ready to serve, push the cocoa through a small fine-mesh sieve to dust the top of the tiramisu.

Serves 12, though it doesn't have to ...

FORGOTTEN PUDDING

There is a wonderful poetry to the name of this dessert which, thankfully, once eaten could never be forgotten. It's an old, old recipe popularly exhumed — I believe — by the late, great Richard Sax. Think of it as a kind of marshmallow-based pavlova. That's to say, you whip egg whites as if making meringue, spread on a jelly roll pan (or that's how I make it), and put in an oven which — as with the moonblush tomatoes on page 126 — you immediately switch off, leaving the pudding to cook overnight — hence, "forgotten."

As for the yolks you don't use: Add a couple of whole eggs to them and make an intensely golden version of the Mexican scrambled eggs on page 230.

6 egg whites	1 cup heavy cream
1/2 teaspoon salt	4 passion fruit
1 1/4 cups plus 2 teaspoons sugar	1 1/2 cups blackberries
1/2 teaspoon cream of tartar	1 1/2 cups quartered strawberries
1 teaspoon vanilla extract	

1 Preheat the oven to 450°F.

2 In a large bowl, whisk the egg whites and salt until peaks begin to form.

3 Gradually add 1/4 cup of sugar, then the cream of tartar and vanilla, whisking all the while at high speed, until the whites are stiff and glossy.

4 Butter a jelly roll pan, then spread evenly with the meringue mixture.

5 Put in the oven, close the door, immediately switch off the oven, and leave overnight, without opening or even thinking of peeking.

6 When you want to serve it, remove to a large platter.

7 Whisk the cream until thick but still soft and spread over the marshmallow-meringue.

8 Scoop out the seeds and pulp of the passion fruit and dot over the cream in parts. Tumble over the blackberries. Toss the quartered strawberries in the remaining 2 teaspoons of sugar and arrange them on the cream, too.

9 Cut into slices; I cut 3 down and 2 across.

Makes 12 squares

against the clock

One of the oft-cited laments of those who don't really enjoy cooking is that a meal takes so much less time to eat than to cook. I don't mind that, not least because I always relish a bit of pottering about in the kitchen; it's the only time I ever get to myself. But also, I have to admit to an affinity to that Victorian worldview, the constant harping on the inevitability of decline — "the woods decay, the woods decay and fall," that sort of thing — and the reminders that all things go back into the earth or up to the heavens. I don't resist the implacable cycle of meals, the kitchen grind.

Luckily, enough of my life is spent on what feels like some sort of cakewalk treadmill for me to have sympathy with those who have a less sentimental attachment to both the kitchen and my fond futilism. There are days, and probably those days are in the majority, when I don't feel I've got more than ten minutes to get supper on the table. Yes, I am willing every now and again to have bread and cheese. I love bread and cheese. But most days I want a proper supper. And I mean "proper." I am not interested in making something easy but dispiriting to eat: As far as I'm concerned every eating opportunity has to be relished, and the idea of wasting one by eating something I don't really want or that doesn't give me pleasure is too hideous to contemplate. It happens, but I am inconsolable after.

Actually, I eat so fast that I'd have thought it would be impossible for me ever to find any recipe that takes less time to cook than to eat, but desperate times need desperate measures — and if an exhausted weeknight, after a 6 o'clock meeting, a row over homework, and a reproachful list of unreturned phone calls and emails doesn't count as desperate times, I don't know what does. I need food I can cook fast or else — not least — I'll eat too much while I'm waiting for supper to be ready. Cook, feed thyself. And indeed I do, on the sorts of foods that follow. These are recipes that are almost too bare-bones to be called that, using ingredients that need at most a quick blitz in a hot pan or a basic, effortless warm-through. They're my fast fallbacks, the sort of meals I can cook when I'm squeezed for time at every angle. In other words, you can do a supermarket sweep at lunch and snatch yourself supper in the evening. And, what's more, the washing up's minimal too.

FLASH-FRIED STEAK WITH WHITE BEAN MASH

When I was a child, steak houses always had something called minute steak, as in *minnit*, on the menu, economically attractive portions that needed a mere 60 seconds to cook through. In our house they were pronounced *mynewt* steaks, as if in baffled disappointment at the meagerness of the meat provided. It's hard to throw off the idea that a steak should be something chunky and big enough to get your teeth into and I certainly like my meat rare. When I'm asked at a restaurant how I want my steak cooked, I tell them just to hit it on the head and walk it straight through. So I can do a proper, fleshly steak supper pretty damn fast, but when you're really up against it, this is the perfect almost-instant dinner. Under five minutes is what I'm talking about from start to finish — and that isn't bad. I could hone it down by sticking to the minute steak idea, and it's fine, only there's something a little school dinners about those sad little straggly rags of steam. This is my compromise: slender but still substantial steak that cooks for 90 seconds a side. And in that time, I've produced a garlicky, lemony, ultrafabulous, utterly addictive bean mash. Below makes enough for four, more if there are children eating too, but I have to come clean and say that I don't quite halve the amounts for the mash when there are just two of us eating. This is just too good, and I simply go down to two cans and a little less of everything else. I'm afraid I don't really want to reduce anything at all.

¼ cup plus 2 teaspoons olive oil	1 sprig fresh rosemary, optional
most of 1 clove garlic, crushed	salt and pepper to taste
grated zest and juice of 1 lemon	4 thin-cut sirloin or entrecote steaks,
3 14-oz cans white beans	about 5 oz each

1 First get on with the beans: Put the ¼ cup of olive oil in a saucepan, mince in the garlic, add the lemon zest, and warm through.

2 Drain the beans and rinse under a tap to get rid of the gloop, then add to the pan and warm through, stirring and squishing with a wide, flat spoon so that the beans go into a nubbly mush. Add the rosemary sprig, if using, and season to taste; some beans come saltier than others.

3 Meanwhile, heat a teaspoon of oil in a large skillet and cook the steaks on high for 1½ minutes a side. Remove to warmed plates, sprinkling some salt and pepper, to taste, over them as you do so.

4 Squeeze the lemon juice into the hot pan and let it bubble up with the meaty oil, then pour over the steaks. Serve immediately with the mash.

Serves 4

Chicken Schnitzel with Bacon and White Wine

It stands to reason that if you want food to cook quickly it needs, first of all, to be fit for the purpose. Thin cuts of meat — and, indeed, fish — are obvious contenders here, but you do have to make sure that speed doesn't take priority over taste. A chicken schnitzel, or escalope, grilled plain is certainly fast fare, but it wouldn't make you skip to the dinner table. Bacon comes to the rescue here; nothing fancy, just sweet, salty ribbons courtesy of Oscar Mayer, which I always keep in the fridge for just such an eventuality.

There's something about the coming together of bacon and white wine that is simple — but ever-compelling. For me, it's the smell, the lure, of carbonara and what it does here is ooze its way through the pan-scorched chicken to make this feel like a treat. And if you can do that with a boneless, skinless piece of chicken breast, you're doing something right.

I love this with some slender green beans — even my children do   and if you have any left over, chop it up and heat with a little cream and Parmesan to make a quick pasta sauce.

1 teaspoon garlic-infused oil	4 4-oz chicken escalopes or boned
4 strips bacon	and skinned breast halves
	1/3 cup white wine

1 Put the garlic oil in a skillet and add the bacon.

2 Fry till the bacon's crisp and the pan is full of bacony juices, remove the bacon to a piece of foil, wrap it, and set it aside for a moment.

3 Fry the chicken for about 2 minutes a side, until there is no pinkness when you cut into a piece. Make sure the pan's hot so that the escalopes catch a little, turning beautifully bronze.

4 Remove the chicken to a serving plate and quickly crumble in the bacon you've set aside, then pour the wine in and let everything bubble up, and pour over the chicken pieces.

Serves 4

HIGH-SPEED HAMBURGER WITH FAST FRIES

I adore a proper burger, but it does need to be a proper one. And although I've been successful in various versions, I've never made one that has been either quick or very convincing-looking. Luckily, my love of gadgetry, combined with my catalogue-compulsion, led to this: the perfect burger, in record time. I use something called, straightforwardly, a Burger Press. You line it with a little disc of waxed paper (these discs come with it) and then put in your 4 oz of meat, put another disc on top, and press. You will not believe how much it makes you want to work in a burger factory.

I had always thought that lean meat made tough burgers, but after much experimentation, I found that the best meat for burgers is one that is sold as "extra lean," which means that it has, typically, a mere 5 percent fat. I use Aberdeen Angus.

The fast fries are not as professional looking as the burgers, but are every bit as satisfying to make. They certainly help you rid yourself of the day's irritations.

8 oz extra lean ground beef	1^1/$_2$ teaspoons soy sauce
1 tablespoon caramelized onions from a jar	1^1/$_2$ teaspoons Worcestershire sauce
1^1/$_2$ teaspoons buttermilk or plain yogurt	good grinding of pepper
	vegetable oil for brushing

1 Mix the ground beef with the onions, buttermilk, soy sauce, and Worcestershire sauce. Season with pepper, then divide in two and form into two patties, either using a press or by hand.

2 Heat a ridged griddle and lightly brush the burgers with oil. Cook the burgers for 2 minutes on the first side, and then flip them and cook them for another minute. Remove and let stand for a minute or two; this will give you medium rare burgers.

3 Serve with the fast fries and sandwich in a toasted bun, if you wish, and add lettuce, melted blue cheese, and bacon or a fried, poached, or squished soft-boiled egg, as you like.

FAST FRIES

^{1}/$_4$ cup vegetable oil	9 oz new potatoes

1 Place the potatoes in a freezer bag and hit them with a rolling pin until they are broken into pieces.

2 Heat a frying pan with the oil until hot, then add the potatoes and cook for 5–6 minutes a side with the pan partially covered.

3 Remove the potatoes to a plate lined with paper towels.

Serves 2

HAM STEAKS WITH PARSLEY

Of course I'm tempted to do a ham steak with pineapple, and I wouldn't begin to stop you, but I really think parsley is the key here. When I've got time, I am happy to stand at the stove whisking up a roux, and stirring, stirring, stirring to usher forth the perfect velvety parsley sauce, but a quick flick of parsley in a pan works in a more sprightly way.

I'm all for peas as an accompaniment, and always have a stash of frozen ones at the ready. Nevertheless, it's hard for me to forswear a can of luridly green marrowfat peas here. Yes, they are processed and I'd prefer not to read the ingredients list on the back of the can, but I can't help loving them. A can or jar of those small, gray-green French peas would be an excellent substitute for those lacking my low tastes. Or cook and drain some frozen peas, blending them with a little Parmesan, pepper, and mascarpone.

2 teaspoons garlic oil	lots of freshly ground pepper
2 cooks' ham steaks, approx. 7 oz each	2 teaspoons honey
2 tablespoons white wine vinegar	1/4 cup roughly chopped parsley
1/4 cup water	

1 In a large-ish skillet, heat the garlic oil and when hot add the ham steaks and cook for about 3 minutes a side. Remove to two warmed dinner plates.

2 Take the pan off the heat. Whisk the vinegar with the water, pepper, and honey and quickly throw into the still-hot pan along with most of the parsley. Swirl and stir and scrape to mix and pour over the ham steaks.

3 Add the vegetable of your choice, in my unembarrassed one the ultragreen processed peas, and sprinkle the rest of the parsley over the two plates of food before tucking in.

Serves 2

MIRIN-GLAZED SALMON

This must be the fastest possible way to create a culinary sensation. You do scarcely a thing — just dip some salmon steaks in a dark glossy potion, most of which you get out of jars — and what you make tastes as if you had been dedicating half your life to achieving the perfect combination of sweet, savory, tender, and crisp.

If there are only two of you eating, I would be inclined to stick to quantities, letting a couple of pieces or whatever you don't eat cool, as it makes a fantastic salad the next day.

My favorite accompaniment here is sushi rice, and since I am wedded to my rice cooker, this is no work and needs no skill whatsoever. Just cook rice of your choice — or noodles if you prefer — according to instructions on the package if you are cruelly rice-cookerless.

1/4 cup mirin (Japanese sweet rice wine)
1/4 cup light brown sugar
1/4 cup soy sauce
4 4-oz pieces of salmon, cut from the thick part of the fillet so that they are narrow but tall rather than wide and flat

2 tablespoons rice vinegar
1–2 scallions, halved and shredded into fine strips

1 Mix the mirin, sugar, and soy in a shallow dish that will hold all 4 pieces of salmon, and marinate the salmon in it for 3 minutes on the first side and 2 minutes on the second. Meanwhile, heat a large skillet on the stove.

2 Cook the salmon in the hot, dry pan for 2 minutes and then turn it over, add the marinade, and cook for another 2 minutes.

3 Remove the salmon to whatever plate you're serving it on, and add the rice vinegar to the hot pan.

4 Pour the dark, sweet, salty glaze over the salmon and top with the scallion strips. Serve with rice or noodles as you wish, and consider putting some sushi ginger on the table, too.

Serves 4

TUNA STEAKS WITH BLACK BEANS

Fresh tuna is good only when it's scarcely, if at all, cooked; once its Carpaccio red flesh turns to that gray mauve, you haven't got dinner in front of you, but a disaster. This, of course, is to our advantage here. Indeed, it takes marginally longer to open a can of beans, drain them, and douse them in dressing than it does to cook the fish. Some tomato salad always works, too; here I've spooned up some leftover Moonblush Tomatoes, of the roughly chopped rather than cherry-halved variety (see page 126).

It's not surprising, then, that I make this very, very often for supper. I get the tuna steaks on my weekly assault on the supermarket and feel just that little bit calmer the minute they're safely in my fridge.

2 teaspoons lime juice	1 14-oz can black beans
1 teaspoon fish sauce (nam pla)	2 tablespoons chopped fresh cilantro
2 teaspoons chile oil	2 thin-cut tuna steaks, approx. 4 oz each
1 teaspoon honey	1/2 teaspoon kosher salt

1 Heat a ridged griddle and while it's heating up, get on with the black bean salad.

2 In a bowl, whisk the lime juice, fish sauce, chile oil, and honey.

3 Drain the beans and rinse them to remove gloop, then toss them in the dressing to coat well. Add most of the cilantro and divide between two waiting dinner plates.

4 Slap the two thin tuna steaks on the griddle and cook for 30 seconds a side. If the tuna steaks are not very thin, you may want to give them another 30 seconds each side; cut into one to check that it's cooked as you like it before placing the tuna on the plate with the beans, adding tomatoes or any other salad you like. Sprinkle the tuna steaks with some coarse salt (not table salt).

Serves 2

SCALLOPS AND CHORIZO

I've long been a fan of scallops and bacon and scallops with chile, and this is my combination of the two, using chorizo — the sausage, not the salami — to ooze its paprika-hot orange oil over the sweet, white scallops. It's quicker than the speed of light to make and quite as dazzling.

4 oz chorizo sausage
1 lb small scallops (halve them to make 2 thinner discs if they are very fat)
juice of half a lemon
$^{1}/_{4}$ cup chopped fresh parsley

1 Slice the chorizo into rounds no thicker than 1/8 inch.

2 Put a pan on the stove to get hot and then dry-fry (the chorizo will give out plenty of its own oil) the chorizo rounds until crisped on either side; this should take no more than 2 minutes.

3 Remove the chorizo to a bowl and fry the scallops in the chorizo oil for about a minute a side.

4 Return the chorizo to the pan with the scallops, add the lemon juice, and let bubble for a few seconds before arranging on a serving plate and sprinkling with lots of parsley.

Serves 4 as a main course with the chickpeas and arugula that follow; would be fine with just a little leafage for 8 as a starter

CHICKPEAS WITH ARUGULA AND SHERRY

This is not quite a stir-fry, though I do cook it in my wok. The chickpeas get soused with the sherry and infused with cumin, and the arugula, or rather tangle of green things that come in the package called "arugula salad" at my supermarket, wilt leggily in the pan. This turns the chorizo and scallops into a feistily elegant main course, and is a useful way of providing a quick, filling bowl of not-the-usual vegetables whenever you want a boost.

1 tablespoon canola or other
    vegetable oil
2 teaspoons cumin seeds
2 14-oz cans chickpeas, drained and
    rinsed

8 cups arugula salad or other tender
    mixed greens
$^1/_4$ cup rich cream sherry
1 teaspoon kosher salt or $^1/_2$
    teaspoon table salt

1 Heat the oil and cumin seeds in a wok.

2 Add the chickpeas, greens, sherry, and salt, give a good stir, and continue stirring over heat until the arugula and any other leaves have wilted, the chickpeas have warmed through, and the liquid has reduced a little.

Serves 4 as an accompaniment to the main course, but you could eat it by itself to serve 2, with or without a poached or squished soft-boiled egg each on top

AGAINST THE
CLOCK

NECTARINE AND BLUEBERRY GALETTE

A galette is just a fancy way of saying "This is a pie, but don't get your hopes up." Not that this isn't good — it's very good indeed — but it is not a perfect specimen. In a way, its raw materials are not so very different from the tarte fine aux pommes on page 217, but whereas there everything is orderly, here it's all thrown together. Suits me.

One half (1 sheet) of a 17.2-oz package all-butter storebought puff pastry, measuring 9¹/₂ x 9¹/₂ inches
1 tablespoon plus 1 teaspoon apricot conserve or low-sugar apricot jam

1 tablespoon plus 1 teaspoon heavy cream
1 small nectarine, cut into 12 segments
²/₃ cup blueberries
1¹/₂ teaspoons Demerara sugar

1 Preheat the oven to 450°F.

2 Lay the puff pastry sheet out onto a baking sheet lined with baking parchment or Silpat and using the point of a sharp knife, score a frame around the edge, about ³/₄ inch in.

3 In a small bowl, mix together the apricot conserve and cream and paint or spread this on the pastry within the frame.

4 Arrange the fruit on top and sprinkle with the Demerara sugar before baking for 15 minutes.

5 Cut into squares and eat while still warm.

Makes 9 slabs

INSTANT CHOCOLATE MOUSSE

Normally, you need to make chocolate mousse a good few hours or, better still, a day, before you want to eat it, so that the egg yolk sets and the whisked whites permeate everything with air bubbles. Forget that: Here we have no yolks, no whites, no whisking, no waiting.

Lack of raw egg, incidentally, also means that you might be happier giving the mousse to small children, though I certainly feel they should not be the only beneficiaries.

1¹/₂ cups mini marshmallows
4 tablespoons (¹/₂ stick) soft butter
9 oz best-quality semisweet chocolate, chopped into small pieces

¹/₄ cup hot water from a recently boiled kettle
1 cup heavy cream
1 teaspoon vanilla extract

1 Put the marshmallows, butter, chocolate, and water in a heavy-bottomed saucepan.

2 Put the saucepan on the stove over fairly gentle heat to melt, stirring every now and again. Remove from the heat.

3 Meanwhile, whip the cream with the vanilla until thick and then fold into the cooling chocolate mixture until you have a smooth, cohesive mixture.

4 Pour/scrape into 4 glasses or small dishes, about ³/₄ cup each in capacity, or 6 smaller (¹/₂ cup) ones, and chill until you want to eat. The sooner the better!

Serves 4–6

CHOCOLATE PEANUT BUTTER FUDGE SUNDAE

I've saved this for last, and for good reason: it is the ultimate ice cream sundae. Obviously, if you're not a peanut-eater, it won't be for you, but for everyone else it is the stuff of dreams. Last time I made this sauce, I nearly had to make another batch, I'd eaten so much before even getting the ice creams out of the freezer.

Talking of which, obviously you should choose whichever flavors of ice cream you want. Even if you are reduced to just plain-old, same old-vanilla, you have a party right here.

I made a jar of this for a friend to take home for her supper recently. As soon as she'd had it she sent a text saying "Bottle that sauce, make millions." Well maybe, but until then, here's the recipe.

And you should know that this is just as irresistible as a storecupboard special, if you replace the syrup and cream with $3/4$ cup of sweetened condensed milk, whisking in $1/4$ cup of hot water from the kettle before pouring the glossy sauce out of the pan.

$3/4$ cup heavy cream	4 scoops toffee or caramel ice cream
4 oz milk chocolate, chopped	4 scoops chocolate ice cream
$1/2$ cup smooth peanut butter (Skippy for preference)	4 scoops vanilla ice cream
3 tablespoons golden syrup or light corn syrup	$1/4$ cup salted peanuts, roughly chopped or left whole, to taste

1 Put all the cream, chopped chocolate, peanut butter, and golden syrup into a saucepan and put it on the heat to melt, stirring occasionally. In about 2 minutes you should have your sauce ready.

2 Get out four sundae glasses and put a scoop of toffee or caramel ice cream in each, followed by one of chocolate and then another of vanilla.

3 Pour over some chocolate peanut butter fudge sauce and sprinkle with salted peanuts.

4 Hand them round.

Serves 4 very lucky people

INSTANT

CALMER

Although I know, from sad experience, that comfort eating does not rely on lengthy preparations, but rather a frenzied assault on the fridge, comfort food cannot easily be rushed. A few ingredients, thrown together in sprightly fashion, can make a fabulous supper, but doesn't guarantee the enveloping coziness we are sometimes hungry for. But I can't ignore the genre; it plays too important a part in life.

It's not hard to think up instant-eating ideas — warm toast, spread with too much butter and a sprinkling of cinnamon and sugar; a family-sized bar of milk chocolate; ice cream straight from the tub; packaged rice pudding — but the comfort they seem to promise is elusive, and one generally ends up hating oneself and feeling sick into the bargain. I want comfort food that really does comfort, that feeds me after a long, difficult day and helps me feel good about life rather than making me want to escape from it.

This, anyway, is the aim. But yes, I do know that some of the recipes that follow are precisely for the sorts of food that I couldn't argue into any kind of diet plan organized by the healthy eating brigade. I can't defend my doughnut French toast from a nutritional point of view, certainly, but I know it has to exist.

These are recipes for the world as it is, for us as we are. I can't always be worrying about how we should be living or eating. I'm hungry now.

CHOWDER WITH ASIAN FLAVORS

This is the perfect supper on those days when a knife and fork seem like just too much work. It's instantly comforting, but is lively enough to make one feel invigorated rather than stultified by eating it. And although to many, replacing the milk with coconut milk, dispensing with the flour and butter, the roux, altogether, and taking the Southeast Asian route rather than the traditional one, might seem an abomination, I love it so much better than the anyway more laborious-to-prepare original.

Children may prefer the lime reduced and the chile removed. I think it is perfection as it is.

3 cups chicken stock/broth (not instant)

1 lb baking potatoes or 2 medium-sized, peeled and cut into $1/4$-inch cubes to make $2^1/2$ cups

4 oz baby leeks, sliced into $1/2$-inch lengths to make 1 cup

4 oz baby corn, cut into $1/4$-inch slices to make $1^1/4$ cups

2 bay leaves

1 teaspoon ground mace

1 14-oz can coconut milk

1 lb 4 oz skinless smoked cod fillets, cut into 1-inch cubes

$1/4$ cup lime juice

8 oz small or medium frozen shrimp

$1^1/2$ cups canned sweet corn, drained

1 teaspoon kosher salt or $1/2$ teaspoon table salt

1 long red chile, deseeded and finely chopped

$1/2$ cup chopped fresh cilantro

1 Bring the stock to a boil in a medium-sized pan. Cook the chopped potatoes, leeks, and baby corn in the stock with the bay leaves and mace for about 10 minutes or until tender.

2 Add the coconut milk, the chopped smoked fish, and the lime juice. Bring the pan back to a boil and let it simmer for a minute or so.

3 Tip in the shrimp and sweet corn and once again let it come back to a boil to heat them through. Season with the salt and then serve.

4 Decorate each bowl with some chopped chile and pungent, leafy cilantro.

Serves 4

NOODLE SOUP FOR NEEDY PEOPLE

I have to say, to be prescriptive about a noodle soup seems to be against the ethos of what you're actually cooking. When I need a noodle soup, believe me I am in no mood to start weighing and measuring. I heat some broth, of some description or other, and throw in a variety of vegetables that are skulking about in the fridge and the most soothing noodles I can find. You can add other things, some chicken strips or, at the end, some fine rags of raw tuna or salmon, but I generally want the vegetably broth and noodles by themselves. The protein element, while so desirable in so many ways I'm sure, is not what I'm after here.

But anyway, I throw down a blueprint here. Don't get caught up in it, but follow it if it feels helpful.

6 oz udon noodles (dried, from a package)

3 cups chicken or vegetable or dashi broth

2 tablespoons soy sauce

1 teaspoon soft dark brown sugar

1 star anise

1 teaspoon minced fresh ginger

$3/4$ cup bean sprouts

$3/4$ cup sugar snaps

$3/4$ cup sliced shiitake mushrooms

$1/2$ cup finely sliced baby bok choy

2 tablespoons chopped fresh cilantro

1 Cook the noodles according to the package instructions and while their water is boiling, fill a nearby saucepan with stock, soy sauce, sugar, star anise, and ginger. (When the noodles are done, just drain them and put half in each bowl.)

2 When the flavored stock comes to a boil, add the vegetables. They should be cooked before 2 minutes are up.

3 Pour half into each bowl, over the cooked and drained noodles, and sprinkle with cilantro.

Serves 2 for supper

Butternut Squash and Sweet Potato Soup

Ever since I overcame my prejudices against buying prechopped fruit and veg, my cooking life has got a lot simpler. And you should know (hope I'm not sounding too defensive here) that Italian grocers regularly sell peeled and prepared vegetables bagged up to make their customers' life simpler.

These squash and sweet potato dice certainly make mine simpler; a quarter of an hour's bubbling with some stock and some spice, and sweet succor is to hand. Sometimes you are not in the mood to wait.

2^1/$_2$ cups diced butternut squash and sweet potato

3 cups hot chicken or vegetable stock

^{1}/$_4$ teaspoon ground cinnamon

^{1}/$_4$ teaspoon ground mace

good grinding of pepper

4 teaspoons buttermilk

1 Put the diced butternut squash and sweet potato in a saucepan with the stock and spices.

2 Bring to a boil, and then simmer for 15 minutes or until the vegetables are tender.

3 Puree the soup in a blender. You will find that by removing the center nozzle on the lid and placing a hand towel or tea towel over the top, you will not get a buildup of pressure and an explosion of soup on your walls or over you.

4 Pour the blended soup into two bowls, decorating each bowl with swirls made with 2 teaspoons of buttermilk.

Serves 2 — or 1 in great need of solace

INSTANT CALMER

Rib-sticking Stir-fry

It's absolutely true that throwing everything in a wok can be a very quick way to get supper on the table, but there are times when what's wanted is something altogether more substantial than the virtuously Oriental culinary traditions allow. There is a good amount of meat — either turkey or chicken, I use both interchangeably — and I throw in a can of cannellini beans rather than going to the, admittedly not really demanding, lengths of cooking and draining some noodles and throwing them in. Curiously, it works. But then, food that can be eaten out of a bowl, with a spoon, always offers succor.

2 tablespoons vegetable oil
10 oz chicken or turkey breast fillet,
    cut into 1¹/₂ inch x ¹/₄ inch strips
4 cups chopped stir-fry vegetables
    (from a package)

¹/₄ cup soy sauce
¹/₄ cup Chinese cooking wine
1 14-oz can cannellini beans, drained
1 tablespoon chopped fresh cilantro
or parsley

1 Heat the oil in a wok, and over fairly high heat add the chicken or turkey strips and toss them about to color.

2 Once the meat has seared, add the vegetables and toss around again until beginning to soften, then add the soy sauce and the wine. The soy will help the meat strips bronze beautifully.

3 Once the heat is back up and sizzling, add the beans and toss everything about to mix before tipping onto two plates.

4 Sprinkle with the herb and serve straight away.

Serves 2

RAPID RAGU

Much to my husband's horror, when I am feeling fragile and in need of coziness and comfort, my favorite supper is a bowl of ground meat with some grated cheese on top, eaten by greedy, grateful spoonfuls out of a cereal bowl.

I have dispensed with much of the usual, necessary chopping: I use cubes of pancetta (or *cubetti di pancetta*, as they're sold at my local supermarket) and a little sweet onion confit from a jar. This is everything you could hope for, sweetly salving and as undemanding to make as it is rewarding to eat.

2 tablespoons garlic-infused oil
1 cup cubed pancetta
1 lb ground lamb
1 14-oz can chopped tomatoes
$^1/_2$ cup water

$^1/_3$ cup Marsala wine
$^1/_3$ cup green lentils
$^1/_4$ cup sweet onion confit
$^1/_2$ cup grated red Leicester or
Cheddar cheese, optional

1 Heat the oil in a wide, medium-sized saucepan, and fry the pancetta until it begins to crisp.

2 Add the lamb, breaking it up with a fork in the bacony pan as it browns.

3 Tip in the tomatoes, water, Marsala, lentils, and caramelized onions and bring to a boil.

4 Simmer the ragu for 20 minutes, stirring occasionally. Sprinkle the cheese on top before serving, if using.

Serves 4

CHICKEN, MUSHROOM, AND BACON PIE

Even the word *pie* is comforting. But then, it would be hard to deny the very real lure of pastry, especially when — as here — you know you're going to dunk it in gravied juices till its gorgeous lightness is deliciously, soggily heavy. I concede, however, that making and rolling out your own pastry is not necessarily the speediest option, so I use bought, all-butter ready-rolled frozen puff pastry and feel fine about it.

I make the pie even easier, by browning the chicken and making the sauce all in one go. And a gold-crusted, welcoming pie for two in half an hour is not bad going.

3 slices bacon, cut or scissored into
   1-inch strips
1 teaspoon garlic-infused oil
2 cups cremini mushrooms, sliced
   into $^1/_4$-inch pieces
12 boneless, skinless chicken thighs,
   each cut into 2- or 3-inch pieces
$2^1/_2$ tablespoons flour

$^1/_2$ teaspoon dried thyme
1 tablespoon butter
$1^1/_4$ cups hot chicken stock
1 tablespoon Marsala wine
Half a 17.2 oz package (one $9^1/_2$ x $9^1/_2$-
   inch sheet) thawed all butter
   ready-rolled frozen puff pastry

1 Preheat the oven to 425°F. Fry the bacon strips in the oil until they begin to crisp, then add the sliced mushrooms and soften them in the pan with the bacon.

2 Turn the chicken strips in the flour and thyme (you could toss them about in a freezer bag), and then melt the butter in the pan before adding the floury chicken and all the flour left in the bag. Stir around with the bacon and mushrooms until the chicken begins to color, about 25 minutes.

3 Pour in the hot stock and Marsala, stirring to form a sauce, and let this bubble away for about 5 minutes.

4 Take two $1^1/_4$ cup pie-pots (if yours are deeper, don't worry, there will simply be more space between contents and puff pastry top) and make a pastry rim for each one – by this I mean an approx. $^1/_2$-inch strip curled around the top of each pot. Dampen the edges with a little water to make the pastry stick.

5 Cut a circle bigger than the top of each pie-pot for the lid, and then divide the chicken filling between the two.

6 Dampen the edges again and then pop on the top of each pie, sealing the edges with your fingers or the underneath of the prongs of a fork.

7 Cook the pies for about 20 minutes, turning them around halfway through cooking. Once cooked, they should puff up magnificently.

Serves 2

CHEDDAR CHEESE RISOTTO

This is the first of my holy trinity of cheese-rich comfort foods. There is just something about melted cheese, that perfect goo, that seems to soothe the soul and bolster the body.

This might seem odd to Italians (one of the reasons it is not in the Hey Presto chapter) but it works beautifully: The starchy rice and the sharp Cheddar are the perfect counterpoint for each other.

I make this, too, on days when I need to escape to the kitchen and have a good, quiet, relaxing, and mindless 20 minutes staring into the middle distance and stirring. I heartily recommend it.

1 tablespoon butter	$1/2$ cup white wine
1 tablespoon vegetable oil	$1/2$ teaspoon Dijon mustard
2 baby leeks or 2 fat scallions, finely sliced	4 cups hot vegetable stock
	1 cup chopped Cheddar cheese
$1^1/2$ cups risotto rice	2 tablespoons chopped chives

1 Melt the butter and oil in a medium-sized pan and cook the sliced baby leeks or scallions until softened.

2 Add the risotto rice and keep stirring for a minute or so, then turn up the heat and add the wine and mustard, stirring until the wine is absorbed.

3 Start ladling in the hot stock, letting each ladleful become absorbed as you stir before adding the next one.

4 Stir and ladle until the rice is al dente, about 18 minutes, then add the cheese, stirring it into the rice until it melts.

5 Take the pan straight off the heat, still stirring as you do, and then spoon into warmed dishes, sprinkling with some of the chopped chives.

Serves 2 as a main course or 4 as a starter

MAC AND CHEESE

How can you have a chapter on comfort food without a recipe for mac and cheese? But I knew there was a fundamental flaw: Making a roux and a white sauce, for the base, is not everyone's idea of having a relaxing time; I realize that my regularly self-administered stirring treatment is not to be prescribed to everyone.

This, then, is the shortcut version: no cheese sauce, but a gorgeously huge amount of cheese, bound with egg and evaporated milk. Yum.

8 oz macaroni	1 cup evaporated milk
2 cups coarsely chopped mature Cheddar or red Leicester cheese, or a mixture of both	2 eggs grating of fresh nutmeg

1 Preheat the oven to 425°F. Cook the macaroni according to the package instructions, drain, and then put back into the hot pan.

2 While the pasta's cooking, put the cheese, evaporated milk, eggs, and nutmeg in a processor and blitz to mix. Or grate the cheese and mix everything by hand.

3 Pour over the macaroni, stir well, and season to taste.

4 Tip into a 10-inch-diameter dish (wide and shallow is best) and bake for about 10–15 minutes or until it is bubbling and blistering on top.

Serves 4

GRILLED CHEESE AND SLAW

By grilled cheese, of course, I mean a grilled cheese sandwich, and I add the slaw, both because I love it and because that way I don't feel so bad about making this for supper. And that's what works for me. Otherwise I'd just have my supper and then this.

Mind you, it is so good that I could never regret it, however tight the dress I might have to wear the next day.

The method is slightly odd, but it's what works for me.

4 slices real white bread, i.e., cut from a loaf
2 teaspoons mayonnaise
1/2 teaspoon Worcestershire sauce
3 oz Cheddar cheese, thinly sliced

1 tomato, thinly sliced
pepper
2 teaspoons regular olive oil (not extra virgin)
Sandwich Slaw, below

1 Heat a ridged griddle pan or stovetop griddle.

2 Get out the bread. Mix the mayo with the Worcestershire sauce and spread on the 4 slices.

3 Now divide the Cheddar and tomato between 2 slices of bread, grind over some pepper, and top with the other 2 slices.

4 Grasping each sandwich in one hand, use the other to dip a pastry brush in the oil and brush the outside of the sandwich with the oil; proceed with the second sandwich.

5 Put the sandwiches on the now-hot griddle and put a skillet on top to weight them, then add heavy cans of soup or jars of pickles or, amusingly, some exercise weights, and grill pinned down like this for 2 minutes a side.

6 Remove to two waiting plates. Serve with slaw, if desired.

Serves 2

SANDWICH SLAW

1 Red Delicious apple, cored and chopped in striplike shapes
1 carrot, cut into matchsticks
2 cups finely sliced or shredded napa cabbage
2 tablespoons mayonnaise

1 tablespoon mango chutney
1 tablespoon lemon juice
1/2 teaspoon caraway seeds
1/4 teaspoon kosher salt or pinch of table salt

1 Put the strips of apple and carrot into a large bowl with the shredded cabbage and toss to mix.

2 In another, small bowl, mix the mayo, chutney, lemon juice, caraway seeds, and salt. Pour this over the salad in the big bowl and mix well to combine and coat before arranging onto the plates of sandwiches.

Serves 2

JUMBLEBERRY CRUMBLE

Since you never know when you might be in urgent need of a crumble, I make up enough for at least four and let it sit safely in the deep freeze until required. Sprinkle over your fruit of choice as it is and cook from frozen. Could scarcely be any easier, could it?

As for the fruit, I take all chopping out of the equation and give it parity with the crumble topping by using frozen mixed summer fruits; "jumbleberry" is just an old English term for whatever mixture of berries were used in jams or puddings or jellies.

FOR THE CRUMBLE TOPPING:
$^2/_3$ **cup flour**
$^1/_2$ **teaspoon baking powder**
4 tablespoons ($^1/_2$ stick) cold butter, cut into small cubes
3 tablespoons Demerara sugar

1 Put the flour and baking powder into a bowl and rub in the cubes of butter with your fingers until you have a mixture like coarse sand. This is such a small amount, it's not really worth getting out the heavy machinery.

2 Stir in the sugar and then put into a freezer bag to freeze.

3 This mixture would make 4 jumbleberry crumbles in the cups (as in the photo to the left), and about 8 ramekins.

TO MAKE ONE CRUMBLE-IN-A-CUP (approx. $1^1/_4$-cup capacity):
$^3/_4$ **cup frozen summer fruits**
1 teaspoon cornstarch
2 teaspoons vanilla sugar or granulated sugar and a drop of vanilla
$^1/_2$ **cup frozen crumble topping**

TO MAKE THE CRUMBLE IN A RAMEKIN:
generous $^1/_4$ cup frozen summer fruits
$^1/_2$ **teaspoon cornstarch**
$1^1/_2$ **teaspoons vanilla sugar or granulated sugar and a drop of vanilla**
3 tablespoons frozen crumble topping

1 Preheat the oven to 425°F. Put the summer fruits in either a cup or a ramekin and sprinkle over the cornstarch and sugar. Stir around a little.

2 Sprinkle over the frozen crumble topping and bake the cup for 20 minutes and the ramekin for 15 minutes.

Serves 1

ROLY-POLY PUDDING

I feel better just contemplating this. You get the comfort of a syrup pudding usually steamed for many, many hours in 30 minutes. And you do practically nothing to make it: Roll out half a 13 oz package of good store-bought pastry, ooze golden syrup over it, roll it up like a jelly roll, and toss it in a dish, pouring on some milk before putting it in the oven.

Eat this with either cream or ice cream: Whatever, it is the perfect Sunday lunch dessert, though there is a good case for it any day of the week.

6 oz store-bought pie crust
3/4 cup golden syrup or light corn
  syrup

1/2 cup whole milk

1 Preheat the oven to 400°F. Roll out the pastry to a size approximately 7 inches x 13 inches.

2 Pour the golden syrup onto the pastry with a 3/4-inch margin around the edge.

3 With a buttered oval gratin dish (11 inches long) at the ready, roll up the pastry from the short side into a fat sausage.

4 Transfer to the dish, putting the seam underneath, and pour half of the milk down one side of the roly-poly and half down the other side.

5 Bake for 30 minutes.

Serves 4 or 1 under certain conditions

BUTTERFLY CAKES

These were the first cakes I ever made as a child — little cupcakes with a disc gouged out of their pointy (or not, and see evidence to the left) tops, cut in two, and the two pieces of cake top set in a blob of buttercream like a pair of butterfly wings. I wasn't much good at making them look like butterflies then, and I see I haven't improved any. The ones here are more bunny buns than butterfly cakes, but they still make me feel strangely comforted. I say "strangely," as there is nothing comforting about the state of childhood. But then, the false solace gained from lying to yourself about the past is probably a necessary evil.

But what am I talking about? Just make the cakes. They're very easy. I whip cream with food coloring rather than making buttercream, and take great comfort in their pretty pastelness.

$^1/_2$ cup (1 stick) plus 1 tablespoon soft butter
$^1/_2$ cup plus 1 tablespoon sugar
2 eggs
$^3/_4$ cup flour
1 teaspoon baking powder
$^1/_2$ teaspoon baking soda
1 teaspoon pure vanilla extract
1 tablespoon milk
1 cup heavy cream
food coloring of your choice

1 Preheat the oven to 400°F and line a 12-cup muffin pan with paper liners.

2 Cream the butter and sugar either in a bowl by hand or with an electric mixer.

3 Once light and fluffy, add the eggs one at a time with a little of the flour, beating as you go.

4 Fold in the rest of the flour, the baking powder and baking soda, and the vanilla, and finally the milk.

5 Spoon the batter into the paper liners, dividing equally.

6 Put in the oven and bake for 15–20 minutes or until the cupcakes are cooked and golden on top. Take the cupcakes in their paper liners out of the pan and let cool on a wire rack.

7 Once they're cool, cut off the mounded peak (if your cakes have obliged), cutting it in half to make the butterfly wings. Dig down a little with your knife. This will also leave a small hole to put the cream to hold the wings. If your cakes haven't peaked much, you will just have to cut out a slightly wider circle after the top, digging in as you do so. As you can see from the pictures, this works just as well.

8 Whip the cream until thick, coloring with food coloring if you wish, and dollop about 2 teaspoonfuls of cream on top of each cake.

9 Stick on your butterfly wings, using the cream as the glue.

Makes 12

Doughnut French Toast

My weaknesses are mainly savory — think salt and potato chips or cheese and crackers — but there are times when only a doughnut will do. This can get desperate late at night when the shops are shut, and even if they weren't, none of them sell the kind of doughnuts I dream of. This is my way of assuaging my appetite, appeasing my need, or, perhaps more accurately, feeding my addiction. Hot chocolate on the side is always worth considering, but just — just! — by itself this is sublime succor.

However, you can, if you like, turn this into a dinner party doughnut-allusive dessert by whizzing up 5 oz hulled strawberries, 4 tablespoons powdered sugar, and a spritz of lemon juice in the blender to make a sauce to pour or puddle over.

2 eggs
$^1/_4$ cup whole milk
4 teaspoons vanilla extract
4 slices from a small white bread loaf or 2 slices from a large white loaf — each large slice cut in half

2 tablespoons butter plus a drop of flavorless vegetable oil for frying
$^1/_4$ cup sugar

1 Beat the eggs with the milk and vanilla in a wide shallow bowl.

2 Soak the bread halves in the eggy mixture for 5 minutes a side.

3 Heat the butter and oil in a skillet, and fry the egg-soaked bread until golden and scorched in parts on both sides.

4 Put the sugar onto a plate and then dredge the cooked bread until coated like a sugared doughnut.

Serves 2

TOTALLY CHOCOLATE CHOCOLATE CHIP COOKIES

Along with chocolate, there is much comfort to be gleaned from reading cookbooks. This recipe combines two loves by being chocolaty to the point of madness and having revealed itself to me after a cozy, snuggled-down read of Elinor Klivans' glorious *Big Fat Cookies*. What I do is make up the full batch of these (hard to divide it really, since it contains only one egg) and form all 12 mounded cookies, but bake only half and freeze the other half. I freeze them in a little shallow pan and once they're hard, I throw them in a freezer bag, seal it, and stash it back in the freezer to bake them unthawed at a later date. That way, I've got 6 chocolate cookies to keep myself and my family happy without any time or effort.

This is what I call an investment. And it's worth it — these are the chocolatiest cookies you will ever come across.

4 oz semisweet chocolate	$^1/_2$ cup light brown sugar
1 cup flour	$^1/_4$ cup granulated sugar
$^1/_4$ cup unsweetened cocoa, sifted	1 teaspoon pure vanilla extract
1 teaspoon baking soda	1 egg, cold from the fridge
$^1/_2$ teaspoon salt	2 cups semisweet chocolate morsels
$^1/_2$ cup (1 stick) soft butter	or dark chocolate chips (2 bags)

1 Preheat the oven to 325°F. Melt the 4 oz of chocolate.

2 Measure the flour, cocoa, baking soda, and salt into a bowl.

3 Cream the butter and two sugars in another bowl. I use my freestanding mixer, itself a source of comfort to me. Add the melted chocolate and mix together.

4 Beat in the vanilla extract and cold egg, and then mix in the dry ingredients. Finally stir in the chocolate chips.

5 Scoop out $^1/_4$ cup-sized mounds — an ice cream scoop and a palette knife are the best tools for the job — and place on a lined baking sheet about $2^1/_2$ inches apart. Do not flatten them.

6 Bake for 18 minutes, testing with a cake tester to make sure they come out semi-clean and not wet with cake batter. If you pierce a chocolate chip, try again.

7 Leave to cool on the baking sheet for 4–5 minutes, then transfer them to a cooling rack to harden as they cool.

Makes 12

Sometimes you have people over for supper, sometimes you have a party. And the trouble is, just because you've planned on giving this party, doesn't mean you have the time to prepare for it. Count yourself lucky. I know that I have perhaps an over-developed antipathy to the formal and fancy, but I do think that not having very much time to do everything does mean you are less likely to go over the top and more likely to throw a party that you and your guests will enjoy more.

The problem with those incredibly detailed, perfectionist-pleasing party plans is that they can reduce the guests to mere cogs in the machine. You're not worried about whether they're having a good time, just whether everything's going according to plan. Sound familiar?

I have nothing against getting out the best china and making the table look beautiful, though I'm rather of the opinion that any table groaning with food is beautiful, crockery be damned. And as for a party that involves standing up and picking at things rather than sitting down and feasting on them, then I agree all effort must be made. But this doesn't mean you have to take two days off work to make the place look the part. I'm all for easy, simple touches. I drape all available surfaces — bookshelves, mantelpieces, side tables — with grapes and assorted fruits, aiming on the whole to evoke the luscious bounteousness of a Roman bacchanalia; I want the guests to be surrounded by fruitful plenty, as if welcoming sumptuousness were just spilling out of every corner.

Flowers, I think, should be present but modest: Don't go in for flashy, expensive displays but rather choose a panoply of smaller flowers that will fit in concomitantly smaller vases. And although I say vases, I mean little bottles, canisters, beakers, and any receptacle that inspires. A case in point: I like to use those small glass pots that fancy French yogurts come in; and, eccentric as it sounds, empty cans — of Italian tomatoes, olives, chestnuts, golden syrup, exotic foreign ingredients, especially when the writing's in a different script — make fabulous vases, particularly in profusion. And I am forever buying odd little jars and containers from eBay to dot about the place with a sprig or two of something beautiful. Remember, it doesn't have to be flowers: Think parsley, rosemary, mint, and any other foliage you can get your hands on. But whatever you use, just bear in mind that what works most is to have as many little pots as possible scattered about all over the place. I rather like going about the house strewing it with fruits and flowers and anything beauteous. It gets me in a party mood.

You need to be practical, too, so remember plates for detritus, ashtrays — sorry to offend the anti-tobacco lobby — stacks of napkins (paper is fine). My mother could never resist finger bowls either, and there is something to be said for filling small dishes with warm water and a slice of lemon, and drop of rosewater too if you're exotically inclined, but on the whole people tend not to use them these days so your thoughtfulness may be wasted and you may be casting pearls before swine, if that's not too rude a way to talk about your friends.

Kingsley Amis once said that the three most depressing words in the English language were "Red or White?" and I think of this every time I throw a party. It was whiskey he wanted to drink, but I don't think you need to supply spirits; just add some other drink that seems to strike a party note. If it's a relatively restrained assembly, in terms of number, this is what I like to get: lots of dry fizzy wine and make sure it is really properly chilled and then lay out a display of flavored syrups, the sort barmen keep behind their bar, and you can pour everyone their wine and let them experiment with the syrup of their choice. My Monin syrups (bought, conveniently, online along with any recherché liqueur I ever need) are beginning to look like some Technicolor army advancing across my kitchen; favorites (with my friends) to splash into the sparkling wine are Rose, Watermelon, Pomegranate, and Passion Fruit. I bring out a different range for Christmas parties (think Cranberry, Winter Berry, Toffee Nut, and Gingerbread, and see pages 316 and 318) and, curious I know, I love them in beer. Speaking of which, if you're serving beer as well at your party, which I think you should if it's summer or if dancing is involved, you must make sure it's so cold it hurts.

As for the food, I never think you should make masses of different things. I think a choice of three, but those three in abundance. Though whatever bits and pieces you do offer people to eat, I think it's always worth baking trays of cocktail sausages in addition. I would feel I weren't giving a proper party without sausages. Putting sausages in the oven and then taking them out again scarcely counts as work either. If you want to make things easier on yourself still, use throwaway aluminum foil roasting pans. I have nothing against dotting the room with bought snacky things, either. You don't have to be embarrassed about serving those rather compelling Japanese rice crackers so long as you're providing real food, too. My absolute favorite are the wasabi-coated peas you can sometimes find in specialty shops, but they do blow your head off, so perhaps they're not for everyone.

Sit-down dinners when you are filled with the desire to do something special but haven't got the time to back it up needn't pose a problem. Again, I think that anything that stops you boning partridges or spinning sugar can only be a good thing. I keep the food simple, but the mood sumptuous. My idea of razzle dazzle is not that you are needily trying to impress everyone, but rather that you are conjuring up an evening that wows with the least amount of work possible.

A final note on the hardest part of any even semi-formal dinner, the *placement*. I hate, hate, hate drawing up seating plans. If you do one, then people are anxious about their position in the pecking order and how they feel it is reflected in the seat you've allocated them; if you don't, they all hover about nervously, not sitting down or knowing what to do, and then you are obliged to produce instant *placement* out of your head. So it's a disaster either way.

This is my way through it all: I number each place and then I fill a hat with another pile of numbers (either buy books of raffle tickets or make your own) and get people to take a number on their way in. This way they know where to sit but don't feel sensitive about their position. If you like to keep things girl-boy-girl-boy — which never worries me, I must say — then just do, as it were, a pink set of numbers and a blue set of numbers and two hats or receptacles by the door. There needs to be a system, even if that system is random. Such is life.

GREEN APPLE MARTINI

This is a cocktail with a kick and addictively delicious. I have to say it is enormously useful as a quick shot of party spirit before you go to someone else's party. I always feel better the next day, having a stiff drink before and water (sparkling rather than still but, hey, let's live a little) during a party.

Although it is a sour apple martini, at home I refer to it only as Kryptonite. The lurid green is quite something.

I've given quantities per glass simply because it's better made up glass by glass and you can hand them around to your guests as they request them. I wouldn't want to make these for a huge roomful of people, but they are perfect as a way of helping those who've hotfooted from the office and are weary with the working day unwind at the beginning of a dinner party. If you want huge pitchers to pass around, either go for the White Lady on page 57 or the gorgeously red Ginger Pom below.

1 shot vodka or gin	¹/₂ shot Monin Green Apple syrup
1 shot sour apple liqueur	slice of Granny Smith apple to garnish

1 In a martini glass, combine the vodka/gin over lots of ice, and add the liqueur and syrup.

2 Slice a segment of apple, removing any core. Cut a nick in the bottom of the slice horizontally, and slip it onto the edge of the glass.

Serves 1 — and how!

GINGER POM

This drink started off as my nonalcoholic alternative for teetotalers (though obviously without the liqueur) and I still do that. But then I came across some pomegranate liqueur and I knew it had a place here. By all means have two pitchers, one with the boozy version, one with just juice and ginger ale, but make sure you and other people can easily distinguish between the two by putting, say, lime slices in the alcohol-free jug. And in either case, make sure this is good and cold.

1 part Pama pomegranate liqueur
2 parts pomegranate juice
2 parts ginger ale

What can I say? Mix these ingredients together and pour over ice.

POTATO CAKES WITH SMOKED SALMON

I've done many versions of potato pancakes in my life, but this has got to be the easiest. I think I shocked myself by making it with instant potato flakes, but there's always got to be a first time. And they taste wonderful, so there is no need to feel bad. But if having an ingredient like this in your cupboard makes you feel too trailer-trash for words, then go to some expensive health-food market and buy a packet of organic potato flakes instead. I do understand.

I have to tell you that if you make these with 1 cup potato flakes and no flour or baking powder, you will have the most stodgily fabulous squat little cakes to eat for break-fast. These are mighty good for soaking up excess, though delicious, fats and juices, although a more elegant version is required here. Serve them at cocktail parties or lay out the component parts, adding a little bowl of crème fraîche or sour cream on the table for an appetizer.

3 eggs
1/2 cup whole milk
2 scallions, finely sliced
2 tablespoons olive oil
3/4 cup instant potato flakes

1/4 cup flour
1/2 teaspoon baking powder
1/2 teaspoon lemon juice
12 oz smoked salmon
small bunch of fresh dill

1 In a batter bowl or similar container, whisk the eggs, milk, finely sliced scallions, and olive oil together.

2 Stir in the potato flakes, flour, baking powder, and then finally the lemon juice.

3 Heat a flat griddle and drop tablespoon-sized dollops of the mixture onto the hot griddle.

4 Cook for about 30 seconds a side or until golden brown and firm enough at the edges to flip.

5 Once you have made the pancakes and they've cooled a little, tear off tiny strips of smoked salmon and arrange the small slices on each pancake.

6 Decorate each salmon-topped pancake with a tiny feather of dill.

Makes 30

THE INSTANT CANAPÉ — QUICK CROSTINI WITH AVOCADO AND GREEN PEA HUMMUS

I love avocados and I've already confessed my *faiblesse* for processed peas, so it stands to reason that one day I was going to try them together. It doesn't sound altogether modest to say this, but it is a triumph. I cannot tell you how quickly these disappear.

Not only is the avocado and green pea hummus a breeze to make, but just to add to your ease, I suggest you use a package of pumpernickel rounds as the crostini base. If you can't get hold of them, just buy a slender French baguette or *ficelle* and slice and so on as on page 239. But the party-pumpernickel should be your first choice.

By all mean use the green-green hummus as a dip if you want, though you'll need lots (add a spoonful or two of cream cheese when mixing too) and serve surrounded with sugar snap peas, sliced sweet peppers, and other crudités of your choice.

It should go without saying that you can replace the canned peas with frozen peas — or indeed fresh — which you cook, puree, and cool before mixing with the avocado. Lovely but not very express.

1 ripe avocado	1 teaspoon kosher salt or $^1/_2$ teaspoon
2 tablespoons lime juice	table salt
$^1/_2$ clove garlic, minced	30 small pumpernickel rounds or 8
2 4.9-oz cans sweet green peas,	regular pumpernickel slices, each
drained	cut into 4 little squares

1 Spoon out the flesh of the avocado and put it in a food processor; add the lime juice and the garlic.

2 Add the drained peas and salt and then process until you have a Kermit colored puree.

3 Spread the pumpernickel rounds softly with the avocado and pea mixture and arrange on a large platter for serving.

Makes 30

TUNA AND CRAB WRAPS

I have never really thought of myself as a person who could wrap, fold, or fiddle about with food or ever felt that way inclined. But you know, when you get into it, it's really quite OK — actually, more than OK. These wraps are curiously relaxing to assemble and everyone is always bowled over by them. They're a very good way of injecting a little zing into the proceedings without having to slave for hours over a hot stove.

I have added the option of the crab wraps as I do understand not everyone is happy working with or even eating raw tuna. But please do try those ones, too: They are actually a very unspooky experience. Just be sure to ask a fish dealer for sashimi-grade tuna and buy it the day you want to eat it.

For both the recipes below I've given the basic unit of wrap; that's to say, amounts are sufficient to fill one tortilla, which in turn will yield 3 pieces once rolled and cut.

FOR THE TUNA WRAPS:

1 teaspoon mayonnaise
$1/2$ teaspoon wasabi paste
1 or 2 drops sesame oil
1 soft flour tortilla
   $1/2$ carrot, peeled and cut into matchsticks to give $1/2$ cup

$1/4$ cucumber, halved lengthways, deseeded and cut into matchsticks to give $1/2$ cup
3 oz tuna-sliced into $1/16$-inch x $3/4$- inch rectangles

1 Whisk together the mayonnaise, wasabi, and sesame oil in a small bowl, and paint the tortilla on one side with this mixture.

2 Arrange a row of carrots horizontally $3/4$ inch–$1^1/4$ inches up from the bottom of the tortilla you have in front of you.

3 Then arrange the cucumber on top of the carrot in the same way, or as best you can, as it may slip down a little.

4 Finally, top with the slices of tuna, also laying them horizontally as this makes it easy to wrap up.

5 Roll up the wrap as tightly as you can, starting from the bottom. You want to end up with a fat Cuban cigar.

6 Cut across the rolled wrap diagonally to make 3 pieces.

FOR THE CRAB AND AVOCADO WRAPS:

$1/2$ cup white crabmeat
1 teaspoon mayonnaise
$1/2$ teaspoon wasabi paste
1 or 2 drops sesame oil

1 soft flour tortilla
$1/2$ avocado
$1/4$ cup finely shredded iceberg lettuce
squeeze of lemon juice

1 Put the crabmeat into a bowl and add the mayonnaise, wasabi paste, and oil and stir to mix.

2 Lay the tortilla in front of you and put the crabmeat in a line horizontally about 1 inch up from the bottom of the wrap.

3 Take the avocado half still with skin and scoop out the flesh in $^1/_2$-teaspoonful curls, laying these on top of the line of crabmeat.

4 Sprinkle over the lettuce in a neat line also, and then spritz with the lemon juice.

5 Roll up tightly from the bottom to form a fat cigar and then slice on an angle into three.

The two recipes combined make 6 pieces

Juicy Beef Skewers with Horseradish Dip

This is another recipe that you can bring into play as something to eat for people who are standing up milling around, or seated at a table as a first course.

I find fresh horseradish incredibly easy to come by these days, but if you don't, use some hot horseradish sauce or cream from a jar.

If you want to serve lamb skewers alongside, then use cubed leg, replace the horseradish in the marinade with a teaspoon each of ground cumin and ground coriander, and make a dip by mixing good store-bought hummus with Greek-style plain yogurt and drizzle the top with a little olive oil before scattering with some pomegranate seeds.

1 lb beef rump
1/4 cup olive oil
3 tablespoons freshly grated horseradish or hot horseradish sauce
2 tablespoons rosemary needles or 1 teaspoon dried plus a bunch of rosemary for decoration, optional
1 1/2 tablespoons good-quality red wine vinegar (otherwise use balsamic vinegar)

2 tablespoons Worcestershire sauce
2 tablespoons port
1 cup crème fraîche or sour cream
1/2 teaspoon Dijon mustard
1/4 teaspoon kosher salt or coarse-grind table salt
1/4 cup chopped chives

1 Cut the beef into 1-inch cubes, and put into a freezer bag with the olive oil, 1 tablespoon grated fresh horseradish or horseradish sauce, rosemary, vinegar, Worcestershire sauce, and port. Set aside for at least 20 minutes, but preferably overnight, in the fridge.

2 Let the meat come to room temperature, and soak about 10 bamboo skewers in water at the same time.

3 Make the dip by beating together the crème fraîche or sour cream and the remaining 2 tablespoons of freshly grated horseradish or hot horseradish sauce with the mustard and salt. Stir in the chives, leaving some chives to sprinkle over the top.

4 Heat a grill or griddle, then thread three or four pieces of meat onto each skewer and slap on the heat, turning after 2 minutes. Cook for another 2 minutes on the other side and then remove to a plate, strewn with some sprigs of rosemary if desired. Do not serve while grill-hot.

Makes approximately 10 skewers

RED-LEAF, FIG, AND SERRANO HAM SALAD

This salad takes mere minutes to make, and yet is so enduringly beautiful. I don't overstate the case; there is something positively painterly about the delicate heaping of dark red leaves, red-bellied figs, and deep pink ham. I love the sharpness of Manchego, dropped in feathery shavings all amongst this, but don't panic if the cheese eludes you (though my supermarket does stock it). Just use some Parmesan or pecorino instead.

1 head radicchio or radicchio rosso

8 cups baby ruby chard or a couple of bags of salad with red-toned tender leaves

2 teaspoons sherry vinegar

2 tablespoons extra virgin olive oil

pinch of salt

8 fresh figs, quartered

10 oz Serrano ham slices, cut very thinly

2 oz Manchego cheese, shaved into slices

1 Tear the head of radicchio into manageable pieces, and toss together with the baby salad leaves.

2 Whisk together the vinegar, oil, and salt in a small bowl and then dress the leaves.

3 Arrange the figs and ham as artistically as you can muster over the salad and then, with a potato peeler, shave the cheese over, letting it fall lightly where it will.

Serves 8

SCALLOPS-ON-THE-SHELL

I can't quite believe how simple but how luscious these are. I prefer to get my scallops from the fish market for this, which is just as well since I don't think I could ever get a supermarket to supply me with shells.

You don't need to take the corals off, but I like to turn this into two meals and fry up the corals the next day with some butter and garlic oil and eat them squished onto chunky bread or toast, spritzed with lemon juice, carpeted with parsley.

These are really a starter, but I certainly wouldn't mind knocking a couple of shells' worth back for a special supper any day of the week.

6 scallop shells
18 sea scallops with their roes or
    corals removed, or if the scallops
    are very small, get 24
2 cups fresh bread crumbs

6 teaspoons butter
1 lime, cut for squeezing
1 1/2 teaspoons garlic oil
salt and pepper to taste

1 Preheat your oven to 475°F. (You really need a very hot oven.) Rinse and dry the scallop shells and arrange them on a baking sheet.

2 Put the scallops into a bowl and sprinkle over the bread crumbs. Toss them around to get each one well coated with crumbs.

3 Put 3 breaded scallops into each shell, and then sprinkle over any leftover bread crumbs that remain in the bottom of the bowl.

4 Then add a teaspoon of butter on top of each scallop-filled shell, a squirt of lime juice, 1/4 teaspoon of garlic oil, and salt and pepper.

5 Put the scallops in the oven for about 15–20 minutes; you really want the bread crumbs to be crispy and the butter turning black around the edges of the shell.

Serves 6

DUCK BREASTS WITH POMEGRANATE AND MINT

This is my idea of perfect dinner-party food: It's easy to make, not complicated to serve, and looks — and tastes — exquisite.

Feel free to broil, pan griddle, or grill your duck rather than sear it on the stove, and then roast it, but I just find I make the air too smoky when it's on the stove.

I advise asking a friend to come and help you slice the meat. Obviously, it's not exactly hard work carving a duck breast, but so that the first slices aren't cold by the time the last ones go on the serving platter, it makes sense to speed up the process. This is not a crucial consideration: It doesn't actually matter what temperature these jeweled slivers of meat are.

4 duck breasts
8 cups arugula or watercress or salad chard or a mixture

1 pomegranate
1 small bunch fresh mint

1 Preheat the oven to 425°F.

2 Heat a flameproof, ovenproof pan on the stove and then sear the duck breasts, skin side down, for a minute or so over high heat.

3 Turn the duck breasts over and then place in the oven for about 15 minutes.

4 Remove the duck breasts from the oven and let them sit on a carving board while you get organized. If you want to hold them at this stage, take them out of the oven at about 13 minutes and double-wrap in aluminum foil, then let them sit till you need them.

5 Line a meat plate or flattish platter with the salad leaves.

6 Slice each duck breast very thinly on the diagonal and lay on the salad-lined dish, pouring over any meat juices as you go.

7 Halve the pomegranate, and then bash out the seeds from one half to decorate the duck slices. Squeeze some of the juice — just by hand — from the other half over the duck as well.

8 Tear off a handful of mint leaves and then finely chop them, scattering over the duck.

Serves 8

GRIDDLED VENISON WITH PINK GIN APPLESAUCE AND ROAST PENCIL LEEKS

There is a certain mellow elegance to this dinner, despite the scant demands it places on you, the cook. I am happy to cook these in a griddle pan rather than roast the venison, since the leanness of the meat means you don't get much smoke, but if you're happier stashing it in the oven, be my guest.

I like to serve this with some pickled red cabbage alongside; its piquancy is the perfect counterfoil to the sweet dense flesh. I don't want anything else, not if I want to make serious headway into any of the desserts below. Nevertheless, consider a good lazy side dish; some really good-quality plain potato chips warmed in the oven is the kind of accompaniment no one, however carb-fearing, can manage to resist.

1¹/₂ lbs venison loin	2 teaspoons black peppercorns
¹/₂ cup gin	1 onion, quartered
¹/₄ cup olive oil	2 star anise
2 teaspoons Worcestershire sauce	2 bruised cloves garlic

1 Put the venison into a large freezer bag and add the remaining ingredients. Leave out for at least 20 minutes, or if you can afford the time up to 2 hours, or leave overnight in the fridge.

2 When you are ready to cook the meat, heat a large griddle pan until almost smoking hot.

3 Take the venison out of the marinade, shaking well, then slap down onto the hot griddle and cook for about 15 minutes, turning frequently to gain even scorch marks. When the venison is ready, remove to a carving board to rest, loosely tented with foil, before slicing thinly.

PINK GIN APPLESAUCE

Don't just buy a jar of applesauce; it's this that makes the venison special. If you own a food mill (and they are not expensive to buy), it's very easy to make.

5 scallions, finely sliced, white part only	3 Red Delicious apples
2 tablespoons butter	2 tablespoons gin plus 1 teaspoon
sprinkling of salt	juice of a lemon
	1 long red chile, left whole

1 In a wide saucepan with a lid, soften the white shreds of scallion in the butter, adding a little salt to prevent it from scorching.

2 Cut the apples in half, and then each half into quarters, and (without even bothering to core) add them to the pan with the scallions. Pour in the 2 tablespoons gin, lemon juice, and whole chile, giving everything a good stir.

3 Cover the pan and cook over medium heat until the apples are soft; this should take no more than 20 minutes.

4 Take out the chile pepper, and then work the sauce through a food mill or sieve, the skins from the apples coloring the sauce a blushing dusky pink. Stir in 1 teaspoon of gin and season to taste.

5 Serve the pink gin applesauce with the venison either in a separate bowl or at one side of the plate of venison.

Serves 6

Roast Pencil Leeks

I love this as a vegetable accompaniment but I should tell you it also works very well, at room temperature, with some dressing over it, as a starter. If you can't find the baby leeks — though there seems to an alarming proliferation of baby vegetables these days — then simply substitute some fat scallions.

> **12 oz miniature leeks**
> **3 tablespoons garlic-infused oil**
> **1 teaspoon kosher salt**
> **juice of $^1/_2$ lemon**

1 Preheat the oven to 425°F.

2 Lay the leeks in a large, shallow baking dish or roasting pan, add the oil and salt, then roll the leeks about to coat well.

3 Cook in the blistering oven for about 15 minutes, by which time they should be bronzed in parts.

4 Decant to a serving dish, and spritz with lemon juice.

Serves 6

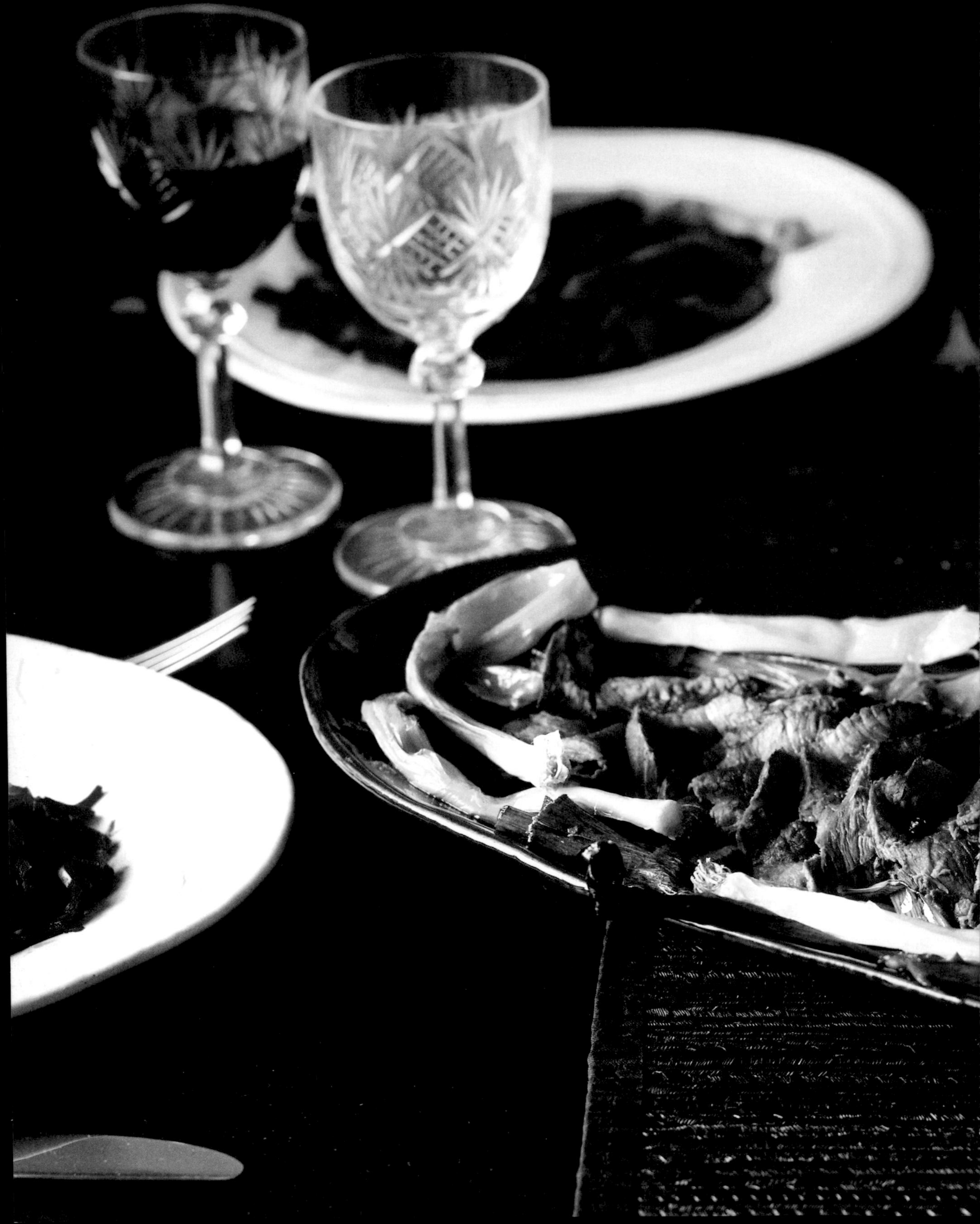

TARTE FINE AUX POMMES

This is the chic version of my lumpy-bumpy galette on page 156. I normally find something fascistically threatening about symmetry, but the lined-up orderliness of this is too beautiful to abhor. Plus, it tastes fantastic and is easy-peasy to make. What more do you want?

2 large Granny Smith apples
   (or 3 smaller ones)
juice of 1 lemon
One half (1 sheet) of a 17.2-oz package
   all-butter storebought puff pastry,
   measuring $9^1/_2$ x $9^1/_2$ inches

2 tablespoons sugar
1 tablespoon butter
crème fraîche for serving,
   if wished

1 Preheat the oven to 425°F.

2 Core the apples, and cut them in half. Pour the lemon juice into a wide shallow dish and fill it with some cold water. Immerse the apple halves in the lemony water; this will stop them turning brown.

3 Lay the sheet of puff pastry onto a large baking sheet, and either using the back of a large carving knife or a steel ruler mark a $^1/_2$-inch border all the way around the edge of the rectangle. You need to score the lines on the pastry rather than cutting all the way through it. This will allow a frame to rise above the apple filling.

4 Pat the apples dry and cut each half into quarters, then slice each quarter as thinly as you possibly can: Think segment wafers.

5 Sprinkle 1 tablespoon of sugar over the base. Working from the inside edge, place the apple slices closely overlapping within the border of the frame. Create neat lines of apple slices until the pastry is covered.

6 Heat the butter with the remaining tablespoon of sugar in a small pan, and let both bubble for a few minutes until a light caramel color appears. Dribble this syrup over the apples and put the tart in the oven.

7 Cook for 20–25 minutes, by which time a puff pastry border will have risen around the apples and the fruit will be soft and slightly colored. Cut into squares or slices and serve with crème fraîche if desired.

Serves 6–8

WHITE CHOCOLATE MINT MOUSSE

I am not normally much of a white chocolate person, but the peppermint seems to eradicate its lethal richness. Nevertheless, my nephew did say of it, when I let him have some for a birthday treat, that it was like being able to eat the icing without having the cake. He wasn't speaking figuratively. And because it is rich and sweet, I serve it in uncharacteristically small portions. As they say in showbiz, always good to leave 'em wanting more.

9 oz white chocolate, broken into small
   pieces
1 cup heavy cream
1 egg white

$^1/_4$ teaspoon peppermint extract (I
   use Boyajian natural peppermint
   flavor)
6 fresh mint leaves, optional

1 Put the pieces of white chocolate in a bowl, and sit this bowl over a pan of simmering water until the chocolate melts, stirring gently with a spatula every now and then. When it's melted, stand the bowl on a cold surface to cool down a little.

2 In another bowl, using an electric handheld whisk for ease, whip the cream, egg white, and peppermint extract together. You want a softly peaking rather than stiff mixture.

3 Put a big dollop of cream onto the slightly cooled chocolate and mix, and then gently fold the chocolate mixture into the rest of the cream.

4 Divide the mixture among 6 small but perfectly formed glasses — like the ones opposite — with a capacity of $^1/_4$ cup each.

5 Chill in the fridge or give them a fast icy zap by sitting them in the deep freeze for 10 or 15 minutes. Decorate each glass with a mint leaf for serving.

Serves 6

RAZZLE DAZZLE

218

GLITZY CHOCOLATE PUDDINGS

If you've got an electric mixer — either a handheld one or a freestanding mixer — this is very low effort indeed, but it is a real showstopper. There's something quite extraordinary about the greedy silence that falls over the table as you put these out. You can almost feel it.

The glitz is provided by their utter fantabulousness and the scattering of candy over the top. If you don't want to use a candy bar, of course, buy some upmarket honeycomb, or else scatter with some finely chopped pistachios. You will lose the sugary-glitter look, but you will still have brought to life an elegantly voluptuous creation.

4 oz bittersweet chocolate
$^1/_2$ cup soft butter
4 eggs
1 cup sugar

$^1/_3$ cup flour
$^1/_4$ teaspoon baking soda
pinch of salt

FOR THE GLAZE:
5 oz bittersweet chocolate
3 tablespoons butter

2 2.1-oz Butterfinger bars, broken into shards

1 Preheat the oven to 350°F.

2 Break up the chocolate and melt it with the butter in a bowl in the microwave or over a double boiler. Once it's melted, sit the bowl on a cold surface so that the chocolate cools.

3 Preferably in a freestanding mixer, beat the eggs and sugar until thick and pale and moussey, then gently fold in the flour, baking soda, and pinch of salt.

4 Fold in the slightly cooled chocolate and butter mixture and then divide among 8 ramekins or custard cups. Put in the oven to bake for 25 minutes.

5 Meanwhile, get on with the glaze by melting the chocolate and butter in a microwave (or double boiler), then whisk to form a smooth glossy mixture and spoon this over the cooked puddings.

6 Decorate with Butterfinger rubble: I just put the bars in a freezer bag, set to with a rolling pin, and strew over the top. Or make this a DIY job by using the Hokey Pokey on page 281.

Serves 8

ICE CREAM CAKE

I don't think a cook's job should be to deceive, but there is something appealing about the fact that this looks and tastes as if it were incredibly hard work and yet involves not more than a bit of stirring. You must, though, serve a warm sauce with it — it's the crowning glory — and I've certainly given you options below.

To be frank, you can choose different cookies, different nuts, and different nubbly bits generally to mix in with the ice cream and give crunch, texture, and sudden shards of flavor. I find it hard to believe, however, that this could be in any way improved. Sorry, but that's just how it is.

$2^1/_2$ pints ice cream
$3/_4$ cup honey-roasted peanuts
$1^1/_4$ cups Nestlé Swirled Milk Chocolate and Peanut Butter Morsels or use chocolate chips of your choice
2.1-oz Butterfinger bar, broken into shards and dusty rubble

$1^1/_2$ cups chocolate cookie crumbs
1 batch butterscotch sauce (see page 27) plus 1 batch chocolate sauce (see page 51) or 1 batch chocolate peanut butter–flavored sauce (see page 160)

1 Let the ice cream soften either in the fridge for a while or out in the kitchen.

2 Line an 8-inch springform pan with plastic wrap, both in the bottom and sides of the pan so that you have some overhang at the top.

3 Empty the slightly softened ice cream into a bowl and mix in the peanuts, 1 cup milk chocolate and peanut butter morsels or chips, Butterfinger shards, and 1 cup of the chocolate cookie crumbs.

4 Scrape the ice cream mixture into the springform pan, flattening the top like a cake. Cover the top with plastic wrap and place in the freezer to firm up.

5 Serve the cake straight from the freezer, unmolding from the pan by releasing the sides and pulling the plastic wrap gently away before putting on a plate or cake stand.

6 Sprinkle the top of the cake with the extra $1/_4$ cup of milk chocolate and peanut butter morsels or chips and the remaining $1/_2$ cup chocolate cookie crumbs.

7 Cut into slices and serve with the butterscotch and chocolate sauces or the chocolate peanut butter–flavored sauce and one of the others, letting both sauces dribble lacily over each slice. If two sauces sound like too much trouble — they're not — just opt for the chocolate peanut butter sauce. It's hard to find an argument against it.

Serves 8–10

BLACKBERRIES IN MUSCAT JELLY

This is unlike anything else: The texture is soft set, so that you know it's not a liquid but it doesn't have the heft of a solid. And the acidity of the blackberries within the musky sweetness of the jelly is a further thrill.

What I do is make this in the morning of the evening I want to eat it. It is so straightforward that you can do it groggily at breakfast, no trouble. It doesn't need so long to set, but I find it easier to work like this.

2 cups blackberries
5 sheets gelatin
2$^1/_2$ cups Beaume de Venise or
    other muscat wine

$^1/_2$ cup water
2 tablespoons lime juice
$^1/_2$ cup vanilla sugar or granulated sugar
heavy cream to serve

1 Divide the blackberries among 6 glasses; I use old-fashioned champagne saucers with a yield of about $^3/_4$ cup each.

2 Soak the gelatin sheets in a dish of cold water for 5 minutes.

3 Put the wine, water, sugar, and lime juice in a saucepan, put on the heat, and stir to dissolve the sugar. Bring to a boil and boil for 1 minute before removing the pan from the heat.

4 Wring out the gelatin sheets and place in a cup. Whisk around $^1/_2$ cup of the hot liquid into the gelatin sheets in their cup before pouring the gelatin and liquid mixture into the pan of hot liquid, whisking well to mix. Allow to cool a little.

5 Pour the liquid over the blackberries in their glasses and refrigerate until set, 3–4 hours depending on how cold your fridge is, or overnight.

6 Serve with some cream in a pitcher, separately.

Serves 6

GINGER-PASSION FRUIT TRIFLE

I don't think I've ever written a book without a trifle in it, and I'm not about to start now. Besides, this is one of those desserts that looks spectacular but requires the least amount of effort and scarcely any time at all to make. And by the way, when I say "make," I really mean assemble.

The taste, though, is glorious and, for all its simplicity of construction, it feels like a big deal. Rich though, which means you can feed a large tableful of people with one fabulous mound.

1 lb store-bought sponge or pound cake or same weight of baker's madeleines
1/2 cup Stone's ginger wine or cream sherry

2 cups heavy cream
4 teaspoons powdered sugar
8 passion fruit

1 Slice or break the cake into pieces and arrange half of them in a shallow dish, then pour half the ginger wine over them. Mound up the remaining half of the cake and pour the remaining ginger wine on top.

2 Whip the cream with the powdered sugar until it is firm but not stiff; you want soft peaks.

3 Scoop the insides of 2 passion fruit into the bowl of cream and fold in before mounding the cream floppily over the drenched sponge.

4 Scoop out the remaining 6 passion fruit onto the white pile of cream so that it is doused and dribbling with the black seeds and fragrant golden pulp.

Serves 8–10

Speedy
GONZALES

This is embarrassing, but I must get it off my chest before I go any further. I do know I am not remotely qualified to tell anyone anything about Mexican food. I haven't, I am both ashamed to admit and regretful to acknowledge, even been to Mexico.

So if it would be misleading to claim this as my Mexican chapter, it is truthful to say it's definitely inspired by Mexican food and culture. Let me just add that I don't actually think that all they eat in Mexico are avocados and tortillas, but somehow they seem to be exuberantly represented here. I have always been someone to keep a regular stash of avocados in the house, but now packages of soft tortillas are as much a staple. If there ain't the wherewithal for a quesadilla in my household, believe me I'm not allowed to forget it.

If I don't claim authenticity, I can at least say that I have endeavored not to be crassly inauthentic. No Mexicans have been harmed in the writing of this chapter. To expand: Wherever possible I have roped in Mexican friends, or friends of friends, to taste, criticize and act as guinea pigs, and their fabulously greedy approval has meant a lot to me.

And while it's true that my delight in the chapter's title might have encouraged me initially, the fact of the matter is my research and the food it inspired in turn have led to some of my favorite recipes in the book. This is not about the lure of the new. I am enough of a traditionalist — in the kitchen at any rate — to be wary of novelty and comforted by the familiar. But this is fast food that is fresh and vibrant and in turn makes you feel more awake and alive eating it.

MEXICAN SCRAMBLED EGGS

This is not only the best way to start the day, but the best way to end it, too. You can make it even more of a meal by serving some refried beans alongside, but I love it just as it is. It also happens to be one of the greatest hangover cures around. You know, I think I might consider overdoing it partywise just to have an excuse to whip up a batch of these. But then, they are so good that there is always a reason to eat them; no need to scout around for excuses.

2 tablespoons vegetable oil
2 soft corn tortillas
1 tomato
1 scallion
**1 small green chile, deseeded and
    chopped**

4 eggs, beaten
**$1/4$ teaspoon kosher salt or pinch
    table salt**

1 Heat the oil in a frying pan. Roll up the tortillas into a sausage shape and then snip them into strips with a pair of scissors straight into the hot oil.

2 Fry the tortilla strips for a few minutes until crisp and golden, then remove to a bowl.

3 Halve the tomato and remove the seeds, then roughly chop it and the scallion and add to the hot oily pan along with the chopped chile, turning everything about for a minute or so.

4 Put the corn tortilla strips back in the pan and add the eggs and salt. Using a wooden spoon, move about in the pan like you would scrambled eggs.

5 Remove the pan from the heat once the eggs begin to set and continue stirring them until they are done to your liking.

Serves 2

MEXICAN CHICKEN SALAD WITH BLACK BEAN SALSA

This is a lunch fit for the gods, and a pretty divine dinner, outside on a balmy night, too.

Jicama is sometimes known as a Mexican potato, though that's a bit misleading since you can eat it raw. It looks like a turnip wrapped in fresh ginger skin. If you can't get hold of a jicama, then I'd replace it with an Asian or Nashi pear or a drained can of water chestnuts, cut into matchsticks; what you want is juiciness and crunch. I wouldn't say no to a Granny Smith apple, cut into chunky matchsticks, either.

I admit I had never even heard of jicama before, but I phoned my greengrocer and he said they were available at the market and just to give him some warning. I don't imagine that you can talk a supermarket into stocking them if they don't already have a leaning toward Latin American produce — though you never know — but I like going to small, specialty stores when I can, and this is another good reason why.

The dressing is utterly addictive. I sometimes keep a jar in the fridge for a day or two; the lime seems to stave off any browning or blackening of the avocado flesh.

FOR THE DRESSING:

1 ripe avocado

$1/2$ cup sour cream

3 tablespoons lime juice

1 clove garlic, peeled

1 teaspoon kosher salt or $1/2$ teaspoon table salt

good grinding of black pepper

FOR THE SALAD:

$2^1/2$ cups shredded cooked chicken

1 lb jicama, peeled and cut into $1/4$-inch matchsticks or 2 8-oz cans water chestnuts sliced into strips

2 scallions, finely shredded

$1/2$ cup finely chopped cilantro

3 cups shredded romaine lettuce

1 Spoon the flesh out of the avocado and put into a blender with all the other dressing ingredients.

2 Process the dressing until smooth.

3 Put all the salad ingredients into a bowl, spoon over the dressing, and toss, making sure everything gets coated well.

Serves 4–6

TOMATO AND BLACK BEAN SALSA

I keep jars of green (milder) and red (hotter) jalapeños, and prefer the fieriness of the red here, but it's entirely up to you. And if you'd prefer to use fresh jalapeños, then do.

1 15- oz can black beans

2 tomatoes, deseeded and roughly chopped

$1/3$ cup roughly chopped pickled red jalapeños from a jar

1 tablespoon lime juice

1 teaspoon Maldon salt or another sea salt

1 Drain and rinse the beans, and then mix in a bowl with the chopped tomatoes, jalapeños, lime juice, and salt.

2 Check the seasoning and then serve with the Mexican chicken salad, either in a bowl to the side or dolloped on the same plate.

Serves 4–6 as part of the meal

Sweet Corn Chowder with Toasted Tortillas

The tortillas before were the soft flour ones. These are those crisp, crunchy corn-gritty triangles that somehow always feel like a guilty pleasure. Although having said that, I know only that "guilty pleasures" exist, but I have never seen the point of feeling guilty about pleasure. Rather, I see plenty of reason for feeling guilty about failing to take pleasure in things.

When I plan to make this, I tend to take a big pack of frozen corn out of the deep freeze at breakfast time, in readiness for a superquick, fantastically soothing, mellow-yellow, and very pleasing supper that night.

Use whatever cheese you like; mostly I go for Cheddar since I always have some in the fridge, but I am happy about using up other bits and pieces. If children are eating, it's wise to omit the chiles — unless they're being *very* annoying.

6 cups frozen sweet corn, defrosted
3 scallions, each one trimmed and
　　halved
1 clove garlic, peeled
$^1/_4$ cup semolina
6 cups hot vegetable stock made from
　　concentrate or bouillon cubes

15 cups lightly salted tortilla chips
2 cups grated cheese
2 long red chiles, deseeded and finely
　　chopped, optional

1 Preheat the oven to 400°F.

2 Drain the corn and put into a food processor with the scallions, garlic, and semolina. Blitz to a speckled primrose mush; unless you have a big processor you may have to do this in two batches.

3 Tip this mixture into a large saucepan, add the hot vegetable stock, and bring to a boil, then turn down the heat and let the chowder simmer, partially covered, for 10 minutes.

4 Meanwhile, spread the tortilla chips out on an alumimum foil–lined baking sheet and sprinkle over the cheese. Warm in the hot oven for 5–10 minutes or until the cheese melts over the chips.

5 Ladle the soup into bowls and put a small mound of cheese-molten chips into the middle of each bowl. Sprinkle over some of the red chile, if you feel like it, and serve immediately to very grateful people.

Serves 6

QUICK CHILI

I suppose this is more Tex-Mex than just Mex, but none the worse for that. Besides, there is a reason that old-fashioned cookbooks devoted so much energy to ground meat: It makes for a simple, speedy supper.

Luckily, there is a lot more going for this than efficiency. It just hits the spot when you want something comforting but not bland: It soothes but it's sprightly.

If you've got a rice cooker — and I make no secret of my dependence here — then you put your rice on to steam before you make the chili and a substantial supper is mere minutes away, which is just the way a substantial supper should be.

5 oz chorizo sausage (not the hard salami sort of sausage), halved lengthwise and cut into $^1/_4$-inch half-moons
1 lb ground beef
$^1/_2$ teaspoon ground cumin
$^1/_2$ teaspoon ground coriander
$^1/_2$ teaspoon ground cinnamon

3 cardamom pods, bruised
2 cups good-quality tomato and chunky vegetable sauce for pasta
1 14-oz can mixed spicy beans
$^1/_4$ cup sweet chile sauce
$^1/_4$ teaspoon chile flakes, optional, or if your canned beans are not spicy

1 Put the sliced chorizo into a hot pan and cook over medium heat until the sausage crisps a little and gives up its orange-red oil.

2 Add the ground beef and cook for about 5 minutes, breaking it up with a wooden fork to help it brown.

3 Stir in the spices and then add the tomato-vegetable pasta sauce, beans, and chile sauce. Also add the chile flakes if you need more heat.

4 Bring to a boil, then turn down the heat and simmer for 20 minutes and eat with rice or just as it is. If you're not adding any rice, you might consider dolloping with a blob of sour cream and sprinkling some grated cheese and chopped cilantro. I can't think of any way of eating this that isn't good.

Serves 4

CHOPPED CEVICHE AND MEXICOLA

I don't deny that chopping the fish into such tiny pieces seems perhaps against the express ethos (if I might put it that way), but there's no logic that can dissuade me. Besides, it really means that you hardly have to steep the fish in the acidy juices at all before it is "cooked" or rather denatured (yes, that is the term) by the lime. Not that that is my reason: I find that eating big chunks of raw fish, no matter that it is cured in some way by its acid bath, can spook people out and this dainty confetti somehow doesn't. I am mad for it and, truth be told, really love it with a big bowl of tortilla chips on the side, but for elegance often produce little toasts or tostadas instead. I get a slender French baguette or *ficelle* loaf and cut into thin slices; one loaf should yield about 40 mini tostadas. Brush with a little oil and then burnish slightly in a 400°F oven for 10 minutes.

Use whatever firm whitefish is available to you; my Mexican sources speak of *sierra* but that's not an option for me, geographically. If I find black cod, sometimes called Chilean sea bass (and is neither cod nor bass), then I use that, otherwise monkfish.

My Mexicola cocktail goes well with this. I can't say I have a rigid formula for this simple drink: I just pour. But I'll jot down what I usually do, per glass, just to get things straight. I put a shot of Tequila into a glass, top with ice cubes, and add lots of lime slices, then fill the glass with very cold Coke or Pepsi.

8 oz skinless and boneless black cod or monkfish fillet, chopped as finely as you can	3 scallions, finely chopped
	¹/₄ cup chopped cilantro, plus a little more for sprinkling
¹/₃ cup lime juice	1 jalapeño chile or any medium-sized green chile, deseeded and chopped to give a tablespoon
1 teaspoon kosher salt or ¹/₂ teaspoon table salt	
¹/₂ teaspoon dried oregano	Tostadas or tortilla chips, to serve

1 Put the chopped fish in a wide shallow dish and sprinkle over the lime juice, salt, and oregano. Leave this for 8 minutes.

2 Drain the fish; it will have made a milky liquid. Add the scallions, cilantro, and chile, and stir gently together.

3 You can either put teaspoonfuls onto little toasts and sprinkle over some more cilantro, or put the ceviche into a bowl for everyone to dip tortilla chips into.

Makes enough for approximately 40 little tostadas

QUESADILLAS

I have been won over to the way of the wrap generally, but I insist this is the best use of the tortilla ever. I came across it first in Miami, in the Raleigh Hotel in South Beach to be precise. The restaurant there is one of my favorites: It nestles in a ludicrously beautiful garden, hung with shimmering lights, and the food is so good that when I'm in Miami I don't dare eat anywhere else.

The Raleigh's Morning Quesadilla is a tortilla wrap, folded around avocado and scrambled egg and grilled and shouldn't by rights be as good as it is. You can do a version of it, should you have any Mexican scrambled egg left over from the recipe on page 230, but I find whenever I put avocado in, it squelches out before I get the wrap to my mouth.

These cheese-and-ham babies are very good to offer alongside the cool ceviche, but I often make them for supper. They're that good — and that easy.

I give quantities for each round soft flour tortilla; each quesadilla makes three little triangles and it's really up to you how many of them to eat. I wouldn't presume . . .

FOR EACH FLOUR TORTILLA WRAP:
1 oz thinly sliced cured ham
3 coin-sliced slices of pickled green
    jalapeño peppers from a jar
¼ cup grated cheese

1 scallion, finely sliced
a few leaves of cilantro
1 teaspoon olive oil (not extra virgin)

TO SERVE:
good store-bought salsa of your choice

1 Heat a ridged griddle, griddle pan, or skillet.

2 Place the tortilla wrap on the counter in front of you and cover with the ham.

3 Over one half only, sprinkle the chopped pickled jalapeño, the grated cheese, and the chopped scallion. Scatter over the cilantro leaves.

4 Carefully fold the tortilla wrap in half, that's to say, fold the un-cheese-topped half over the cheese so you have a fat half-moon.

5 Lift this up carefully and brush each side with the oil before putting it on the hot griddle; grill each side for a minute.

6 Using a steady hand and a wide fine spatula or fish slicer, transfer the tortilla to a board or plate and cut into three triangles. Eat with some salsa on the side. And please feel free to play with the fillings as you wish.

Makes 1 quesadilla

Roquamole

I have practically had to sit on my hands to stop myself writing about this before now. Now, naturally I know Roquefort does not come from Mexico, but because it melds deliciously with avocado I couldn't resist; I hope you won't be able to, either. And although I have called this incredible dip roquamole, I think it may be better made with a less illustrious *bleu*. Saint Agur out of a wedge-shaped package is the cheese I keep in the fridge so that I am ever-ready to make this.

You don't need to serve blue corn tortilla chips with this; you don't have to serve any kind of tortilla chip with this, though both do add to the luscious eat-me quality here. But I'm also very keen on a huge platter of dippable bits: radishes, carrot batons, sugar snaps, you name it.

For me, this can be a dip with drinks, a quick treat for lunch, or a greedy solitary dinner. The only meal I've yet to eat it at is breakfast. I think it's just a question of time ...

1 cup crumbled Roquefort or Saint
    Agur blue cheese
$^1/_4$ cup sour cream
2 ripe avocados
$^1/_4$ cup sliced pickled green jalapeños
    from a jar

2 tablespoons finely sliced scallions
$^1/_4$ teaspoon paprika
large bag of blue corn tortilla chips

1 Crumble or mash the blue cheese with the sour cream in a bowl.

2 Mash in the avocados. If they are ripe, a fork should be all you need.

3 Roughly chop the sliced jalapeños and stir them into the mixture along with the finely sliced scallions.

4 Arrange in the center of a plate or dish, dust with paprika, and surround with tortilla chips. Dive in.

Serves 4–6

FLAN

This is a ridiculous simplification of a traditional Mexican dessert that is no less delicious for being easier to make. You don't always have to suffer for your art.

In effect, this is a large crème caramel; there's nothing to stop you making it as many smaller, individual ones, but it will take longer to line each mold. Why give yourself the work? The fact that the flan takes around three-quarters of an hour doesn't bother me. You don't need to be doing anything while it bakes and anyway it needs a good long time to sit around and chill. But you can do likewise while that's happening.

The traditional method is to make a kind of milk reduction; I know that opening cans does sound a bit like trailer trash cooking but in essence, you've just let someone else reduce the milk for you. I find this particular combination of unsweetened evaporated milk and sweetened condensed milk does the trick, so discard your prejudices and arm yourself with your can opener.

A Mexican camera assistant, Luis, I worked with once says this is as good as his mother's. I only hope his mother doesn't know.

³/₄ cup sugar	3 large eggs
1 12-fl-oz can evaporated milk	2 teaspoons vanilla extract
1 14-oz can sweetened condensed milk	

1 Preheat the oven to 325°F and put a kettleful of water onto boil.

2 Put the sugar into a heatproof, heavy-bottomed, or ideally copper tarte tatin dish (or 9- inch-diameter pie tin), and place over low heat until the sugar begins to turn into a liquid syrup. Swirl the sugar every now and then as it melts.

3 The sugar will begin to caramelize — just before the sugar reaches the color of maple syrup, take the pan off the heat and place it on a cool surface.

4 While the pan's cooling down a little, swirl the caramelized sugar a little up the sides of the dish before it sets.

5 Empty the evaporated and condensed milks into a bowl and whisk in the eggs and vanilla extract.

6 Pour this mixture over the syrup-lined tarte tatin dish and put it into a roasting pan, filling the pan with freshly boiled water to about 1 inch full.

7 Bake for 45–50 minutes or until firm and set. Lift the dish carefully out of its water bath and set aside to cool.

8 Leave the flan in the fridge overnight or for 4 hours. When you are ready to serve, turn the flan out onto a dish with enough of a lip on it to stop the syrup running off.

Serves 8–10

MARGARITA ICE CREAM

This is a cinch to make, and easy-easy-easy to eat. It is, now that I come to think of it, in effect a no-churn version of the ice cream in *Forever Summer*. If you want to serve it in glasses dipped in sugar and salt, by all means do. But it is so good that even as someone who is not a committed ice cream eater and no kind of a drinker, I find I can spoon it straight into my mouth from the container I've chilled it in.

In other words: No decorative touches or embellishments are remotely needed. This is truly the express way to dessert-deliriousness.

¹/₂ cup lime juice	1¹/₄ cups powdered sugar
3 tablespoons Cointreau or triple sec	2 cups heavy cream
2 tablespoons tequila	

1 Pour the lime juice, Cointreau (or triple sec), and tequila into a bowl and stir in the sugar to dissolve.

2 Add the cream and then softly whip until thick and smooth but not stiff.

3 Spoon into an airtight container to freeze overnight. This ice cream does not need ripening (softening before serving), as it will not freeze too hard and melts speedily and voluptuously.

Serves 6

Buñuelos

A buñuelo is a small fritter of intense fabulousness. I think anything that is fried starts off with an advantage in the taste department, and a good sprinkling of sugar at the end can only help things further.

Although these are fried, they are incredibly light, and the oil you cook them in is very hot, so that the buñuelos do not have even the suspicion of greasiness about them.

If you have a freestanding mixer — which generally greatly aids the express life — these are very quick to make, and they take hardly any time to fry. I love them at the end of a meal with a small, hot cup of coffee.

If you want to take an even more express route, simply cut some soft corn tortillas into triangles, deep-fry them quickly but ferociously, and then sprinkle with a goodly dusting of powdered sugar.

$^1/_4$ cup milk	$^1/_8$ teaspoon cream of tartar
1 egg	1 tablespoon vegetable shortening
1 cup flour	cooking oil for frying
1 teaspoon baking powder	powdered sugar for decorating

1 Whisk the milk and egg in a large measuring cup or bowl.

2 Put the flour, baking powder, and cream of tartar into a bowl, then rub the shortening into the mixture either by hand or with a freestanding mixer.

3 Pour in the milk and egg and mix to make a silky dough; be prepared to add 1–3 tablespoons of extra flour if it's too sticky.

4 Pour the oil in a pan up to about 1 inch deep and place over high heat to reach a temperature of 350°F.

5 Tear off cherry tomato–sized balls from the dough, rubbing them with your hands to shape them. Drop into the hot oil and cook for about 1 or 2 minutes on each side or until golden.

6 Drain on paper towels and then arrange on a plate and dust with powdered sugar pushed through a small strainer with a teaspoon.

Makes 30; enough for 4–6 or 8 if just a petit four with coffee

MEXICAN HOT CHOCOLATE

This is not the first of my Mexican hot chocolates, but I feel it will be my last. You can melt chunks of chocolate (as I have in previous versions) into hot milk, but I love the particular richness and thickness you get from good European hot chocolate powders. Plus, I add Kahlúa, so there is really no need to consider anything else.

The whipped cream on top is not essential unless you decide to serve this in lieu of dessert-and-coffee, which I can't help thinking is a very, very good idea indeed.

Canned whipped cream, which gives that glorious whipped effect is, alas, not always wonderful, but if you're brave enough, buy a nitrous cream whipper and learn to spurt and squirt the fresh cream at will.

2 cups whole milk
6 tablespoons superior European hot
   chocolate mix
$^1/_4$–$^1/_3$ cup Kahlúa, depending on
   taste

squirty whipped cream from a can,
   optional
4 long cinnamon sticks

1 Heat the milk in a pan and make the hot chocolate according to package instructions.

2 Add the Kahlua and then take off the heat before it boils.

3 Serve with a topping of the squirty cream (if you are using), and put the cinnamon sticks in as you would straws, though I am not suggesting they be used as such.

Serves 4

have never seen any point in pretending to be other than one is, and I do rather feel anyway I have made the most of being a food obsessive. For good or bad, it's my life, it's me, and I don't see anything changing. Sometimes, though, I do have the good taste to be a little ashamed. So, I risk showing myself up in all my foolishness now by confessing that when my son started having to take a packed lunch to school every day, I kept a diary, chronicling what I'd given him to eat and — oh yes — memorializing either his comments or the state of his lunch box by the end of the day. In other words, I told myself, I was trying to see what was successful and popular and what went uneaten.

I realized how madly obsessive I was being when all my friends derided me for charting the princeling's prandial progress in this fashion; not knowing I was so idiotic, you see, I just left the diary in plain sight in the kitchen for ease of jotting.

Well, it didn't last (the abandoned document now languishes in my secret drawer) not just because I was mocked, but also because the novelty wore off, to be frank. But what I do know from all that is how hard it is to supply decent lunches, day in, day out, for adults or children, or even just something to eat on the go, when the food has to travel, sit well, and be prepared without major trauma. The recipes that follow represent my attempt to find a way through it all. Follow me . . .

PEA AND PESTO SOUP

Providing something hot to eat is the hardest challenge, and although thermos flasks of soup provide scope for spillage and mess, I feel they are worth the risk. This soup — my all-time most-requested— has the bonus, too, of being so simple to make, you can do it while you stumble about the kitchen at breakfast.

While you *can* make it with pesto from a jar, the difference when you use the "fresh" stuff in a plastic tub that you find in refrigerated sections in the supermarkets is astonishing.

I think soups taste better made in a blender rather than a food processor, and it's best to use a blender with a lid that has a central bit in the top you can remove; this stops pressure building up, which in turn prevents you from getting soup all over you or your walls. This would not be a good start to the day.

3 cups water	1 teaspoon kosher salt
3 cups frozen peas	$^1/_2$ teaspoon lime juice
2 scallions, coarsely chopped	$^1/_4$ cup fresh pesto (not jarred)

1 The quickest way to proceed is to fill a kettle first and put it on to boil. When it's boiled, measure the amount of water you need into a pan and put on the stove to come back to a boil.

2 Add the frozen peas, scallions, salt, and lime juice and let everything bubble together for 7 minutes.

3 Discard the scallions and blitz the peas and their liquid with the pesto in a blender.

4 Pour into a thermos flask that you've left filled with hot water and then emptied and make sure you screw the top on securely.

Makes enough for 2 hearty bowls

CHICKEN CAESAR CORNETS

This is a wrap by another name, but for a reason: There is no way I think a roll-up wrap could survive travel but this, a kind of crepe-cornet approach, is hardier. You'll still have to be careful, but at least you start with an advantage.

I love these so much, I have to be careful not to eat everyone's packed lunch when I make them.

1 heaped cup shredded, cold cooked
    chicken
¹/₄ cup organic mayonnaise
minced or crushed garlic, optional
²/₃ cup Parmesan cheese shards

2 cups chopped iceberg lettuce
¹/₄ teaspoon Worcestershire sauce
salt and pepper to taste
4 soft corn tortillas

1 Put all the ingredients, except the tortilla wraps, in a bowl and mix well.

2 Place a tortilla on the counter in front of you and spoon a quarter of the mixture onto a quarter of the wrap. Fold the wrap in half, and then in quarters, so a flat, doubled side covers the bulgy filled side, and proceed with the remaining three tortillas.

3 Wrap well in aluminum foil before traveling.

Makes 4

ROCKY ROAD CRUNCH BARS

No one is ever going to complain about having one of these in their lunch box, and they're pretty handy to have around in the kitchen for a quick, snatched burst of energy at any time.

I'm not claiming them to be a health food, but when you're talking about lunch on the run, packing quite a few calories into a small parcel can be viewed as a positive advantage. That's my view, and I'm sticking to it.

1/2 cup (1 stick) plus 1 tablespoon soft butter

10 oz semisweet chocolate, broken into pieces

1/4 cup light corn syrup

8 oz plain hard and crunchy cookies, such as Nabisco Social Tea Biscuits

2 cups mini marshmallows

2 teaspoons powdered sugar

1 Melt the butter, chocolate, and corn syrup in a heavy-bottomed saucepan. Scoop out about 1/2 cup of this melted mixture and set aside.

2 Put the cookies into a freezer bag and then bash them with a rolling pin. You are looking for both crumbs and pieces of cookies.

3 Fold the cookie pieces and crumbs into the melted chocolate mixture, and then add the marshmallows.

4 Tip into a 9-inch-square aluminum foil pan and flatten as best you can with a spatula. Pour over the reserved 1/2 cup of melted chocolate mixture and smooth the top.

5 Refrigerate for at least 2 hours or overnight.

6 Cut into 24 fingers and dust with powdered sugar by pushing it gently through a small fine-mesh sieve or tea strainer.

Makes 24

SESAME PEANUT NOODLES

I always make a large vat of these since they're lovely to keep to pick at in the fridge, too. Plus, although they're easy to make, you do need quite a few ingredients — and this holds true whether you're making a small or big batch, so you may as well go all out.

FOR THE DRESSING:

1 tablespoon sesame oil

1 tablespoon garlic-infused oil

1 tablespoon soy sauce

2 tablespoons sweet chile sauce

$1/3$ cup smooth peanut butter

2 tablespoons lime juice

FOR THE SALAD:

$1^1/_4$ lbs cooked egg noodles

2 cups bean sprouts, rinsed

$1^1/_2$ cups snow peas

1 red pepper, seeded and cut into small strips

2 scallions, finely sliced

$1/_4$ cup sesame seeds

$1/_4$ cup chopped fresh cilantro

1 Whisk together all of the dressing ingredients in a bowl or small pitcher.

2 Put the noodles, bean sprouts, snow peas, sliced red pepper, and sliced scallions into a bowl.

3 Pour over the dressing and mix thoroughly to coat everything well.

4 Sprinkle with the sesame seeds and cilantro and pack up as needed.

Serves 8

BANANA BUTTERSCOTCH MUFFINS

A great portion of my life is spent baking with bananas. I don't know that I would have actively chosen this path, but since I haven't been able to shake off my inability to throw food away, ever, I am ineluctably driven to find ways of salvaging bananas too ripe to be easily eaten raw. It's hard to resist the lure of these muffins, and they are incredibly quick and easy to mix up and bake. Furthermore, their resilient squidginess makes them very good travelers.

White chocolate morsels can be used in place of the butterscotch ones and my children seem to love both with equal fervor, though I'm pretty fond of these with dark chocolate chips, too.

$\frac{1}{2}$ cup vegetable oil

2 eggs

$1\frac{2}{3}$ cups flour

$\frac{1}{2}$ cup sugar

1 teaspoon baking powder

$\frac{1}{2}$ teaspoon baking soda

$1\frac{1}{4}$ cups mashed bananas (2–3 ripe bananas)

1 cup butterscotch (or chocolate) chips

1 Preheat the oven to 400°F and line a 12-cup muffin pan with paper liners.

2 Measure the oil into a large glass measuring cup and beat in the eggs.

3 Put the flour, sugar, baking powder, and baking soda into a large bowl and mix in the liquid ingredients, followed by the mashed bananas.

4 Fold in the butterscotch chips, then divide equal quantities into the waiting muffin pan — I use an ice cream scoop and a spatula — and bake in the preheated oven for 20 minutes.

Makes 12

CRUNCHY SALAD WITH HOT AND SOUR DRESSING

As with the sesame peanut noodles, this is one of those salads I love to have around to pick at from the fridge, and unlike the noodles, it is the very model of low-cal virtue. But because it's got such powerful flavors, such bite, it feels more filling and substantial than it has the right to be. It really keeps you going, which can be useful halfway through a long day at work.

FOR THE DRESSING:

2 tablespoons rice vinegar

2 tablespoons canola oil

1–2 teaspoons Tom Yam paste
(according to taste)

1 teaspoon sesame oil

1 teaspoon honey

sprinkling of kosher salt

FOR THE SALAD:

2 cups broccoli florets cut into 1-inch
pieces

1 cup quartered slender green beans

1 cup baby corn, each cob cut into 4

2 cups finely shredded napa cabbage

2 cups bean sprouts

1 cup button mushrooms, sliced

1 Whisk together the dressing ingredients in a glass measuring cup.

2 Cook the broccoli florets with the fine beans and baby corn for 2 minutes in a pan of boiling water. Drain and refresh them by plunging them in a sink or tub of cold water.

3 Put the shredded cabbage, bean sprouts, and sliced mushrooms into a bowl and add the drained and refreshed vegetables.

4 Dress the salad, tossing everything together well.

Serves 4–6, depending on whether you're eating this as lunch in its entirety or as a side dish

LUNCH BOX TREATS

This is exactly what it says in the title: crunchy, crisp, sweet, and toothsome, and the really good thing on top of all that is that, as a parent, you feel you are doing your children good while at the same time giving them a treat. The amount of milk chocolate is scant, and I get a warm rush from considering the nutritional benisons of malt, oats, and sesame seeds.

$1/2$ cup rice malt syrup
$1/4$ cup butter
2 oz milk chocolate
2 cups crispy rice cereal

1 cup cornflakes
$1/2$ cup quick-cooking oats (not instant oatmeal)
$1/2$ cup sesame seeds

1 Melt the syrup, butter, and chocolate gently in a heavy-bottomed saucepan.

2 Add all the other ingredients, turning to coat everything well.

3 Using your hands (encased in latex gloves), shape the mixture into walnut-sized balls. You should get about 25; you could also make this using a 12-cup muffin pan with paper liners to get 12 cupcakes.

4 Let them set in the fridge for an hour or so, and they will keep quite happily in there for a week of treats.

Makes 25 treats or 12 cupcakes

MORTADELLA PASTA SALAD

I have a certain amount of ambivalence about pasta salads, but find that my emotional seesaw tips ever more in favor of them. Truth is, I used to be scathing. But finding them so popular with my children makes me see their virtues.

This one is a favorite at home, though none of my finicky lot want the green bits; if you suffer the same irritations and constraints, take out the parsley and leave it for adults to sprinkle optionally.

8 oz fusilli pasta

2 tablespoons extra virgin olive oil

2 tablespoons lemon juice

1 teaspoon kosher salt or $1/2$ teaspoon table salt

$1/2$ teaspoon mild German mustard, or similar

1 thick slice mortadella in 1 piece, about 5 oz, diced into $1/4$-inch pieces to give 1 cup

$1/2$ cup finely chopped curly parsley, optional

$1/3$ cup Parmesan cheese, flaked

1 Bring a pan of water to a boil, add salt to taste, then cook the pasta according to the package instructions.

2 Meanwhile, whisk together the oil, lemon juice, salt, and mustard to make the dressing.

3 Drain the cooked pasta and tip it into a large bowl, pour over the dressing, and toss well to coat.

4 When cool stir in the mortadella pieces, chopped parsley (if using), and Parmesan. Check the seasoning, adding salt and pepper as required.

Serves 4 as a packed lunch

MINI MEAT LOAVES

Make these, eat them, and you'll see how glorious they are; I know only too well that they don't look so good. But let's not go into that. I find these not only delicious, but a real boon to boot: I can make up a whole batch and freeze the ones I don't want to dispense immediately. This is a wonderful time-saver.

These mini meat loaves are best eaten cold, either dunked in mayo, ketchup, or mustard, or sliced and made up into sandwiches with the whole fandango of sauces. I sometimes add some lingonberry to the mix, too. Throw in a gherkin and some pickles and this is lunch nirvana. Don't forget the napkins, though.

1 lb sausage meat
1 lb ground beef
1 cup quick-cooking oats (not instant oatmeal)
$^1/_3$ cup A.1. Steak Sauce

2 eggs, beaten
2 teaspoons Worcestershire sauce
1 teaspoon kosher salt or $^1/_2$ teaspoon table salt

1 Preheat the oven to 400°F.

2 Combine all of the above in a bowl, mixing really well with your hands or a fork.

3 Divide the mixture into 12 balls, and then shape them into mini loaves.

4 Sit the mini meat loaves on a baking sheet with space between them and cook for 30 minutes.

5 You could eat them hot, but best let them cool and keep in the fridge to slice and eat in sandwiches.

Makes 12

SPANISH OMELETTE

There's something about a chunky golden triangle of potato-and-pepper-filled omelette that makes a packed lunch or picnic feel sunshine-filled and cheery. This is easy enough to make, but you do need to get it done in advance as the hottest you want to eat this is room temperature.

It is often decreed that the only ingredients (other than the eggs of course) proper to a Spanish omelette are onions and potatoes, but I like a little touch of olé red with some chopped peppers. Use either the confetti dice of roasted red peppers that comes in jars, or buy a jar of whole roasted ones and roughly chop them yourself.

I am sorry if this offends — and not only the Spanish — but you could speed this up by using some drained, canned new potatoes instead of cooking real ones.

8 oz baby new potatoes, halved
4 eggs
1/2 cup grated Manchego or Cheddar
   cheese
1/3 cup chopped roasted red peppers
   from a jar

3 scallions, finely sliced
salt and pepper to taste
1 teaspoon butter
drop of oil

1 Turn on the broiler and let it heat up while you start off the omelette.

2 Cook the new potatoes in boiling water for 15 minutes until cooked through, then drain.

3 Whisk the eggs in a bowl and then add the cheese, pepper, and scallions and season with salt and pepper.

4 Heat the butter and oil in a small skillet, and once hot pour in the omelette mix and cook gently for 5 minutes.

5 By this time, the bottom of the omelette should be set and rather than turn it, simply sit the skillet under the broiler for a few minutes to set the top.

6 Turn the omelette upside down onto a plate to let cool. Don't worry if it feels a little wibbly-wobbly in the middle, as it will carry on cooking as it cools.

7 Once cool, slice into 4 large or 8 smaller wedges.

Serves 4 or more, depending on what else is available to eat at the same time

ON THE RUN

BUTTERMILK ROAST CHICKEN

Buttermilk chicken has long been one of my favorite al fresco summer suppers. My method of choice has usually been to butterfly a chicken — or rather, many chickens — and then cut them into feisty quarters to layer up on serving plates. I've altered this to make cooking speedier, and conveying easier, by using only drumsticks.

12 chicken drumsticks (approx. 3 lbs total weight)
2 cups buttermilk
1/4 cup plus 2 tablespoons vegetable oil
2 cloves garlic, bruised and skins removed

1 tablespoon crushed peppercorns
1 tablespoon kosher salt or 1 1/2 teaspoons table salt
1 teaspoon ground cumin
1 tablespoon maple syrup

1 Place the chicken drumsticks in a large freezer bag, and add the buttermilk and 1/4 cup of oil.

2 Add the bruised garlic cloves to the bag with the crushed peppercorns and salt.

3 Sprinkle in the ground cumin and finally add the maple syrup, and then squish everything in the freezer bag around to mix the marinade and coat the chicken.

4 Leave the buttermilk-marinated chicken in the fridge ideally overnight or out of the fridge for at least 30 minutes and up to 1 hour.

5 Preheat the oven to 425°F. Take the chicken pieces out of the bag, shaking off the excess marinade, and then arrange them in a roasting pan lined with aluminum foil.

6 Drizzle over the 2 remaining tablespoons of oil, and then roast in the oven for about 30 minutes, or until brown, even scorched in parts, and juicily cooked through.

Serves 6

New Orleans Coleslaw

This is my accompaniment of choice for the buttermilk chicken. Indeed, I have even converted fiercely committed anti-coleslawers with it. I can't remember why I call it my New Orleans Coleslaw now (I've been making it, or a version of it, for so long), but I think it has something to do with all the wonderful pecan trees I saw when I was there.

Do serve a potato salad alongside if you want: You see, in the picture on page 275 you see some baby new potatoes doused in olive oil, salt, and a little lime juice, shaken about in a mustard jar.

1 head of white or savoy cabbage, weighing about 2 lbs before trimming
2 carrots
4 scallions
2 stalks celery
1 cup best-quality, preferably organic, store-bought mayonnaise
$^1/_4$ cup buttermilk
2 tablespoons maple syrup
2 teaspoons apple cider vinegar
salt and pepper to taste
$^2/_3$ cup pecans, fairly finely chopped

1 Trim and shred the cabbage; you can do this either by hand or with a food processor.

2 Peel and grate the carrots, and finely slice the scallions and celery. Toss all the vegetables together in a bowl.

3 Whisk together the mayonnaise, buttermilk, maple syrup, and vinegar and coat the shredded vegetables with this dressing.

4 Season to taste with salt and pepper and toss in the chopped nuts.

Serves 6

CLOUDY LEMONADE FOR A SUNNY DAY

I am thinking that carrying a pitcher of lemonade out into the yard or garden counts as portable food, and since I am always, always in a hurry I am no doubt on the run. You could, of course, pour this gloriously simple, old-fashioned lemonade into a thermos flask and take it on your way.

If the mood takes you, you could consider adding a handful of raspberries to the blender jar to create pink lemonade.

4 cups chilled club soda or other carbonated water
2 whole unwaxed lemons, cut into eighths

$^1/_4$ cup superfine sugar, or to taste
ice cubes

1 Put the water, lemons, and sugar into a blender in two batches, and blitz until the lemon is pureed.

2 Sieve the lemonade into a pitcher, pressing down into the sieve, and then pour into tumblers filled with ice.

Serves 4–6

ON THE RUN

HOKEY POKEY

I was going to say that this isn't as fun as it sounds, but then I reconsidered. Hokey pokey is the Cornish term for honeycomb, and is wonderful eaten in golden shards or crumbled into the best vanilla ice cream. You can also use it in place of the Butterfinger bars on pages 221 and 222. I include it here as it is the perfect present to take to a dinner party. Better than flowers, as they need to be put into a vase, better than chocolate, which people tend to smile politely at, but put away in a drawer: No one can resist a bit of Hokey Pokey, I've found.

The quantities I've specified don't make an awful lot — enough to fill a little tin about $4^1/_2$ inches in diameter and $2^1/_2$ inches deep — but any more and you'd be sued by your dentist.

$^1/_2$ **cup sugar**
4 tablespoons dark corn syrup
1$^1/_2$ teaspoons baking soda

1 Put the sugar and syrup into a saucepan and stir together to mix. You can't stir once the pan's on the heat, though.

2 Place the pan on the heat and let the mixture first melt and then turn to goo and then a bubbling mass the color of maple syrup — this will take 3 minutes or so.

3 Off the heat, whisk in the baking soda and watch the syrup turn into a whooshing cloud of aerated pale gold. Turn this immediately onto a piece of reusable baking parchment (Silpat) or greased aluminum foil.

4 Leave until set and then bash at it so that it splinters into many glinting pieces.

Makes 2 cups

Hey PRESTO

I have spent a lot — a majority now, come to think of it — of my adult life pretending to myself that I am Italian. Well, maybe "pretend" is the wrong word: I know I am not really, but feel myself to be. But since I have the misfortunate not to be Italian in reality, I must be entitled to one — the only one surely — of the advantages. And that is, I can play a little fast and loose with Italy's culinary traditions. I respect them, I love them, but what — truly — would be the point of giving you here the respected and loved recipes that centuries upon centuries of Italians have been cooking as tradition decrees? Part of me would indeed love to do just that (and I have some plans, simmering away on a back burner, that might permit such a thing in the distant *futuro*), but for now I wanted to be as faithfully Italian as I could in my reworking of recipes, while not feeling I had to be slavishly authentic.

This isn't necessarily about cutting corners; one of the great attractions of much Italian cooking is its speed, directness, and simplicity. But I do know also that many Italian friends of my generation and younger don't cook, feeling that their lives are more frenetic and work-dominated than the lives their parents and grandparents lived. The recipes that follow attempt to make Italian food manageable, and easily manageable, after a long day at the office — and I've used an Italian journalist friend as a guinea pig to make sure that I've succeeded in that, without offending real live Italians.

I've twiddled and fiddled a little, because that's what makes cooking alive. I love this sort of food, and playing around with it in the kitchen is always a lifter of the spirit. The hardest thing has been whittling down this chapter so it doesn't take over the whole book. So know that what follows is the backbone of my repertoire and the recipes I just couldn't, couldn't live without. Hope you feel the same way.

TUNA AND BEANS

This has always been *the* Italian antipasto but although traditionally you are more likely to come across it as the combination of *tonno* and cannellini, I love the flecked terra-cotta of cranberry beans, giving you the colors of Tuscany on a plate.

And if you are feeling less formally Italianate in mood, then this makes a simple, speedy supper for two; all I'd want alongside is some good bread.

$1/3$ cup finely chopped red onion	2 tablespoons extra virgin olive oil
$1/4$ cup lemon juice	salt and pepper to taste
2 14-oz cans borlotti or cranberry beans	2 tablespoons chopped parsley
1 8-oz can best-quality tuna to give $1^1/4$ cups	

1 Put the chopped onion into a bowl with the lemon juice and let it steep while you get on with the salad.

2 Drain the beans and rinse them to get rid of any gloop, then arrange them in a bowl.

3 Drain the tuna and flake it into the beans.

4 Add the olive oil to the onion and lemon juice mixture and whisk to make a dressing, pour this over the tuna and beans, and transfer to your serving dish.

5 Fork the salad through, seasoning with salt and pepper, and then scatter over the parsley; if you want to put this on a plate (rather than a dish), consider strewing the plate with arugula first, or using it to make a leafy border.

Serves 4–6 as a starter or as part of a meal

MOZZARELLA WITH CRAZY GREMOLATA

There are no bad ways of eating good mozzarella. I am perfectly happy just with a sprinkling of salt and a green glug of olive oil, but this is something special. Gremolata — or gremolada — is the traditional flavoring spritz given to osso buco, and is a sprinkly mixture of grated lemon zest, garlic, and parsley. Mine, here, is an exuberant, madcap version, full of fire and flavor and gorgeously vibrant against the milky white of the mozzarella.

2 balls buffalo mozzarella
1 long red chile, deseeded and finely chopped
6 black olives, finely chopped
zest of 1 unwaxed lemon

$1/2$ clove garlic, minced
$1/2$ teaspoon kosher salt or $1/4$ teaspoon table salt
3 tablespoons extra virgin olive oil
2 tablespoons finely chopped parsley

1 Slice the mozzarella into $1/4$-inch rounds and arrange them on a plate.

2 In a bowl, mix the chopped chile with the chopped olives, lemon zest, and minced garlic.

3 Tip in the salt, oil, and parsley and stir together to make your c-c-c-c-razy gremolata.

4 Spoon the gremolata down the center of your sliced mozzarella.

Serves 6 as part of a starter

PAPPARDELLE WITH ESCAROLE

This is as simple and as basic as a recipe could be, and all the better for it. I love the way Italians cook greens with their pasta, and often those are the recipes, perhaps thought to be unglamorous, that don't make it over here. And maybe it's also the case that non-Italians need a little more persuasion to throw a lettuce into their saucepan. If you can't get escarole, which is a member of the endive family, use any similar lettuce — curly endive, frisee, or some such. What you want is a robust leaf with an edge of bitterness, and with it I think you need an equally robust pasta. I always go for the thick rough ribbon of pappardelle, but failing that, you might consider rigatoni.

1 tablespoon garlic-infused olive oil
1 teaspoon dried crushed chiles
16–18 cups roughly sliced escarole
1 cup white wine
1 cup water
1 lb egg pappardelle

$^1/_2$ cup chopped parsley
$^1/_2$ cup flaked Parmesan cheese
salt to taste
1 long red chile, deseeded and finely
    chopped, optional

1 Put a large pot of water onto boil for the pappardelle.

2 In another — wide — pan, heat the oil gently with the dried chile flakes, and then add the sliced escarole, stirring to help it wilt down in the oil.

3 Add the wine and water and partially cover the pan, letting the escarole cook, bubbling away, for about 6 minutes and let the pasta cook in its pan at the same time.

4 Toss the drained pasta into the cooked escarole (this will be a fairly liquid mixture) and scatter with the parsley and cheese, checking the seasoning as you do so; decorate the top with the fresh red chile if you want enhanced heat and color.

Serves 4–6

LINGUINE WITH LEMON, GARLIC, AND THYME MUSHROOMS

This is one of my proudest creations, and I suppose a good example of a recipe that isn't traditionally from Italy, but sits uncontroversially in her culinary canon. I don't think it would be too presumptuous to name this *linguine ai funghi crudi*. It is about as speedy as you can imagine: You do no more to the mushrooms than slice them, steep them in oil, garlic, lemon, and thyme, and toss them into the hot cooked pasta. I'm afraid I had to have this forcibly taken away from me during the photo shoot for this book, otherwise I'd have eaten it all up before it had even had its picture taken.

The dressed mushrooms also make a great salad, but in which case boost the quantities of sliced mushrooms (keeping other ingredients the same, and obviously you're omitting the pasta altogether) to 6 cups.

If all you can find are regular button mushrooms, this pasta is still worth making — so no excuse for not.

8 oz/4 cups finely sliced cremini
   mushrooms
1/3 cup extra virgin olive oil
1 tablespoon kosher salt or 1 1/2
   teaspoons table salt
small clove garlic, minced
zest and juice of a lemon
4 sprigs fresh thyme, stripped to
   give 1 teaspoon leaves

1 lb linguine
1 bunch parsley, chopped to give 1/2
   cup
2–3 tablespoons freshly grated
   Parmesan cheese, or to taste
freshly ground pepper

1 Slice the mushrooms finely, and put them into a large bowl with the oil, salt, minced garlic, lemon juice and zest, and gorgeously scented thyme leaves.

2 Cook the pasta according to the package instructions and drain loosely, retaining some water. Quickly put the pasta into the bowl with the mushroom mixture.

3 Toss everything together well, and then add the parsley, cheese, and pepper before tossing again, and eat with joy in your heart.

Serves 4–6

SPAGHETTINI WITH SHRIMP AND CHILE

This is what I make for people when I want something that needs no thought, no fuss, no effort but will guarantee instant gratification all around. I keep the shrimp in the deep freeze and either thaw them overnight (or more likely from breakfast time till after work) in the fridge, or do a quick thaw job when I get home. The sunblush tomatoes are generally stashed in my fridge to spruce up salads, make up a quick sauce, or gussy up pasta just like this.

1¹/₂ cups frozen cooked peeled shrimp, defrosted	2 tablespoons garlic-infused oil
salt	1 cup sunblush tomatoes in seasoned oil
8 oz spaghettini	¹/₂ cup white wine or Noilly Prat
¹/₄ cup finely sliced scallions	1¹/₂ cups arugula
¹/₂ teaspoon crushed chile flakes	¹/₄ cup chopped flat-leaf parsley

1 Drain the shrimp and leave to one side for the moment.

2 Put on copious amounts of water to boil, then when boiling add salt and then the pasta and cook according to package instructions, or slightly under.

3 In a large pan (big enough to take the pasta later), fry the finely sliced scallions and chile flakes in the garlic oil for a couple of minutes, then tip in the tomatoes with their oil and the shrimp.

4 When both have warmed through, add the white wine or Noilly Prat and let bubble up. Add the arugula, torn roughly, and stir till wilted a little.

5 Strain the pasta when ready, reserving half a cup or so of pasta-cooking water, and toss the drained pasta in the chile-shrimp pan.

6 Turn out into a large warmed serving bowl and toss everything again so that all is combined, adding a little of the cooking water if it needs it and adding more oil or garlic oil if you want.

7 Sprinkle with the chopped flat-leaf parsley, and serve.

Serves 4 as a starter, 2 as a main course

BLACK PASTA WITH RED MULLET

While it's true that colored pasta — even the impeccably authentic black squid pasta — is eaten very much more out of Italy than within it, this recipe is inspired by the most wonderful fish pasta I had the summer before last at a small restaurant, La Fontanina, on the road that spirals up from Porto Santo Stefano on the Tuscan coast. I tend to make this as a special treat, as supper for two, but if you want to, of course serve it as a starter, but go light, very light, afterward.

I use rosé wine, because that's what I drink — clinked with ice and spritzed with soda — throughout summer, but white would be fine, and much more Italian to boot.

I've indicated the pasta I customarily use (and buy from the supermarket) as it is much more tender than the dried squid pasta. But please, use any tender, thin ribbons of pasta you want. And if red mullet is not available, northern goatfish or red porgy are the best alternatives. Bass would be a lovely but expensive option.

2 tablespoons garlic-infused oil	good grinding of pepper
2 scallions, finely sliced	2 tomatoes, halved, deseeded, then
7–9 oz red mullet, goatfish, or red	chopped into dice
porgy fillets	2 tablespoons drained capers
1 cup rosé wine	1 tablespoon butter
½ teaspoon kosher salt or ¼	8 oz fresh black squid tagliolini
teaspoon table salt	⅓ cup basil leaves

1 Put a saucepanful of water on to boil for the pasta.

2 Heat the oil in a skillet and cook the scallions for a minute before adding the fish fillets, skin side down.

3 Turn the fillets over after a minute or 2, then pour in the wine and add the salt and pepper.

4 Once the fillets are cooked through, which should be in about another minute, lift them out and wrap in aluminum foil to keep warm.

5 Let the winey pan juices bubble down for about 3 minutes, then tip the tomato dice, capers, and butter into the pan and whisk on the heat.

6 Cook the fresh pasta — it will take about 2 minutes — and drain it, put it into the sauce, then toss gently but well.

7 Flake the fish, leaving the red skin on parts, and tenderly toss through the pasta with the basil, leaving some more to sprinkle on when you serve.

Serves 2 as a main course, 4 as a starter

POLLO ALLA CACCIATORA

This is an old favorite — chicken cooked "the hunter's way" — which grants a certain amount of culinary license. This, my version, is traditional enough, only speeded up and simplified. The only unexpected deviation lies in the addition of a can of cannellini beans. This, in effect, turns it into a quick, one-pot, all-inclusive supper. Having said that, I also adore it — as do my children — with plain steamed rice as well. But whatever, when I cook this, I know I can count on getting supper on the table from scratch comfortably in under half an hour.

1 tablespoon garlic-infused oil	$^1/_2$ teaspoon celery salt
$^1/_2$ cup pancetta cubes	$^1/_2$ cup white wine
6 scallions, finely sliced	1 14-oz can chopped tomatoes
1 teaspoon finely chopped fresh rosemary	2 bay leaves
	$^1/_2$ teaspoon sugar
1 lb chicken thigh fillets, each cut into 4 pieces	1 14-oz can cannellini beans, optional

1 Put the garlic oil into a pan with the pancetta, sliced scallions, and chopped rosemary and fry for a couple of minutes.

2 Add the bite-sized chicken pieces, stirring well, and sprinkle in the celery salt.

3 Pour in the wine and let it come to a bubble before adding the tomatoes, bay leaves, and sugar. Put the lid on and let the pan simmer for 20 minutes.

4 Drain and add a can of cannellini beans (if using), and when they have warmed through too, you are ready to eat.

Serves 4

LAMB RIB CHOPS WITH CHILE AND BLACK OLIVES

No one does lamb chops better than the Italians and this recipe, which comes to me by way of the great Anna Del Conte, is a case in point. The nuggets of pink meat are so tender and flavorful, you just want to gnaw every morsel right off the bone.

I'd keep side dishes plain — maybe some steamed new potatoes and green beans or some such — as this needs no attention-seeking embellishment.

And I can't tell you how heavenly they are, should you be lucky enough (and it's unlikely) to have some left over, snatched cold straight from the fridge the day after.

12 lamb rib chops
1/4 cup olive oil
3 cloves garlic, peeled and sliced
1 teaspoon chile flakes
1 teaspoon dried oregano
zest and juice of 1 small lemon

1 teaspoon kosher salt or 1/2 teaspoon table salt
15 black olives, pitted and sliced
2 tablespoons oil, for frying
1 long red chile, deseeded and finely chopped, optional

1 Layer the rib chops between plastic wrap and flatten them gently with a rolling pin or meat mallet. Place the chops in a large dish so that they all fit in a single layer.

2 Pour over the 1/4 cup of oil and add the garlic, chile, oregano, and lemon zest and juice. Sprinkle over the salt and the olives and then turn the rib chops in the marinade so that both sides are coated.

3 Cover and leave the lamb to marinate for 20 minutes at room temperature before cooking.

4 Heat a large skillet with the 2 tablespoons of oil and add the chops, scraping off the marinade before you put them in the pan. Fry them for a couple of minutes a side on quite a high heat so that they take on some color.

5 Turn the heat back down to medium and pour the marinade into the pan over the colored chops. Add 2 tablespoons or so of water so that they cook in a little liquid. Cook for about 5 minutes for rare cutlets or a little longer if you like your lamb well cooked (this will also depend on the thickness of the chops).

6 Transfer the lamb to a serving plate, pour over the juices from the pan, and sprinkle with the chopped red chile should you feel like enhancing the dried chile with the pep of fresh.

Serves 4

LIVER WITH BACON AND CHARRED ONIONS

Liver is not for everyone, I admit, and I wouldn't advise cooking it for a dinner party. But those who love it, adore it, and it makes a great treat for a supper for two. Liver and onions is as Italian as it is British (though very different) and I add bacon to this, as the salty juices are the perfect frying medium for the liver, adding foil and counterpoint to its moussey, sweet flesh. I like to keep the tones beautifully somber; with the scorched dark pink of the bacon are splintered sweet strands of blackened red onion, and with the liver — as homage to *fegato alla veneziana* and because the fresh bitterness is just what's needed — I make a salad of maroon-leafed radicchio.

If you feel like enhancing the renaissance painting atmosphere, consider scattering some pomegranate seeds on top.

4 slices bacon

1 teaspoon garlic-infused oil

1¹/₂ cups thinly sliced half-moons of red onion

12 oz very thinly sliced calf's liver, about 4 long, thin pieces

2 tablespoons balsamic vinegar

2 tablespoons water

1 tablespoon chopped parsley

1 Cook the bacon in the teaspoon of garlic oil until very crisp, and then remove to paper towels and then to a piece of aluminum foil, wrapping the slices into a baggy but tightly sealed parcel to keep warm.

2 Cook the onions in the same pan — in the rendered bacon fat — until soft and wilting and beginning to char in parts, and then remove them to a bowl.

3 Cook the liver in the same pan again, for about 1¹/₂ minutes a side or longer if it hasn't been very thinly sliced.

4 Divide the cooked liver between 2 plates and quickly wash out the pan with the vinegar and water, letting it bubble up and make a scant syrup.

5 Pour this over the liver and cover with the onions. Crumble over the bacon and sprinkle with the parsley.

Serves 2

ITALIAN SAUSAGES IN HOT TOMATO SAUCE WITH POLENTA

Italian sausages are fabulously quick to cook — and fabulously good to eat. And if the lamb chops on page 299 provide just the right sort of heat for a spring or summer meal, these sausages blanket you with winter warmth. The heat they are draped in comes from a couple of jars of really top-quality tomato and chile pasta sauce. A regular pasta sauce just won't cut it here; it has to be a genuinely impressive high-end one.

1 tablespoon chile oil
2 lbs Italian sausages, sweet or spicy
4 tablespoons Marsala wine
2¹/₂ cups chile tomato sauce for
    pasta

1 cup water
1 lb instant polenta
boiling water and chicken stock
    concentrate or bouillon cubes
2 tablespoons olive oil

1 Heat the chile oil in a skillet and add the sausages, separating the links and letting them fry for about 5 minutes until they are colored.

2 Add the Marsala and let the pan bubble for a minute or so, then pour the tomato chile sauce and water over the sausages.

3 Simmer for 15 minutes while you get on with making up the instant polenta according to package instructions only using chicken stock (from a bouillon cube or concentrate) rather than just water.

4 When the polenta's cooked, whisk in 2 tablespoons of olive oil. Divide the polenta among 6 warmed plates and top with the sausages and hot tomato sauce. If you have more sauce than you need per plate, just pour it into a little pitcher for people to add as they want.

Serves 6

MARSALA-HONEY PEARS WITH GORGONZOLA

With all due respect to de Gaulle and his countrymen, I would happily forgo each and every one of France's 246 cheeses for one wedge of Gorgonzola. For me, it is the king of cheeses, the queen of cheeses, the grand empress of cheeses. This dish is my way of paying respects to it, although I admit I am perfectly happy to eat it all alone (just me and the cheese). If you want cheese at the end of a dinner party, then this is the way to do it.

And while it's not an Italian recipe, it is entirely Italian in inspiration. For me it's autumn in Milan cast in food.

2 pears (approx 1 lb total weight), each cut into eighths (but unpeeled and uncored)
2 tablespoons olive oil (regular, not extra virgin)
3 tablespoons Marsala wine
2 tablespoons honey
$^1/_2$ cup walnut halves
1 lb ripe gorgeous Gorgonzola in perfect condition; it should never have seen the inside of your fridge

1 While you are cutting the pears into eighths — i.e., quarter them and halve each quarter — let the oil heat in a large skillet.

2 Fry the pears for 3 minutes a side, and while they are frying whisk the Marsala and honey together in a cup.

3 When the pears have had their time, throw in the Marsala-honey mixture and let it bubble up vociferously around the pears. Then transfer them, all bronzed and syrupy, to a plate.

4 Add the walnuts to the dark juices left in the pan and stir-fry them for about a minute until they are themselves darkened in part and sticky all over. Remove them to the plate with the pears and add ingredient X, your Gorgonzola.

Serves 6–8

PEACHES IN MUSCAT

The Italians have a way of making a special dessert out of unmessed-up simple ingredients. It's something to do with their touch. I mean — take *affogato*, which is just a scoop of vanilla ice cream "drowned" by having a strong hot cup of espresso thrown over it. Or there's *sgroppino*, which is a scoop of sorbet in a glass, topped up with a fizzy hit of Prosecco. Dessert can be entirely store-bought and still feel like a treat: You just buy a bottle of Vin Santo and provide cantuccini biscuits to dunk in.

And I love the way they make fruit feel special too, just by washing grapes, cherries, and apricots and sitting them in bowls of ice water directly on the table. This recipe is scarcely more work, and if you don't want to do any of it in advance, then just put a bottle of Muscat wine on the table and a bowl of peaches, give everyone a sharp knife and a glass, and let them pour their own Muscat and slice in their own peaches.

> **4 ripe peaches**
> **1 cup sweet Muscat wine or other good dessert wine**
> **heavy cream or ice cream for serving, optional**

1 Over a bowl (to catch juices), cut each peach into slices.

2 When all the peaches are sliced, pour in the Muscat wine and make sure the peaches are more or less fully immersed. Cover the bowl with plastic wrap and refrigerate for up to 6 hours; sometimes it helps to be able to get stuff done in advance.

3 Remove the peaches to a pretty glass bowl or to individual small glasses and serve — still chilled — with a pitcher of heavy cream or some vanilla ice cream alongside.

Serves 6

AMARETTO SYLLABUB

This is really an Anglo-Italian hybrid: The syllabub is entirely English, though the liqueur used makes it Italian in the extreme. The crumbled amaretti biscuits give a trifle-like contrast of soaked cake and soft cream. Utterly delicious, and with the moments it takes to make, this is something you can pull out any time you want to end a dinner party with aplomb.

$^1/_3$ cup Amaretto liqueur
2 tablespoons sugar
1 tablespoon lemon juice

1 cup heavy cream
1 8-oz package *amaretti morbidi* (soft almond macaroons)

1 Pour the Amaretto liqueur into a bowl with the sugar and lemon juice and whisk to mix.

2 Whisk in the heavy cream and whip this mixture until it has thickened but is still soft and billowy.

3 Crumble 2 little amaretti cookies into each of the 4 glasses (each with a yield of about $^2/_3$ cup).

4 Divide the syllabub among the glasses on top of the crumbled cookies.

5 Crumble another macaroon or two, and sprinkle this golden rubble over the top of all the glasses to give a fine sprinkle of crumbs on each. Serve the remaining amaretti alongside the syllabub.

Serves 4

BUDINO DI CIOCCOLATO

This is chocolate pudding by another name, but somehow it sounds better in Italian. But frankly, language is irrelevant here: We're talking pure, all-encompassing bliss. When you eat it cooled, it is like chocolate satin cream and almost shocking in its pleasurable intensity, but I love it, too, hot and straight out of the pan when it is like the best hot chocolate you've ever had, in spoonable form.

1 cup whole milk	2 tablespoons boiling water
1/2 cup heavy cream	2 egg yolks
1/3 cup sugar	1 teaspoon vanilla extract
1 tablespoon cornstarch	2 oz dark chocolate, finely chopped
1/3 cup cocoa	

1 Put the kettle on to boil water, and warm the milk and cream together either in a saucepan or the microwave.

2 Put the sugar and cornstarch into another saucepan and sift in the cocoa. Add the 2 tablespoons of boiling water and whisk to a paste.

3 Then whisk in the egg yolks, 1 at a time, followed by the warmed milk and cream, and then the vanilla extract.

4 Scrape down the sides of your pan and put it on the heat, cooking and whisking for about 3–4 minutes until the mixture thickens — if it helps, think of a consistency like mayonnaise.

5 Take off the heat and whisk in the finely chopped chocolate before pouring into 4 small cups or glasses each with a yield of about 2/3 of a cup.

6 Cover the tops of the cups with plastic wrap, laying it directly on top of the pudding to stop a skin from forming, and then refrigerate once they are cooler. Make sure they are not still fridge-cold when you serve them. You can add a blob of cream on top if you like. And see the cookies on the next page.

Serves 4

CHOCOLATE MACAROONS

You don't have to serve these *amaretti scuri* with the *Budino di Cioccolato* but I had to do something with the egg whites left over from the pudding and this is it. I love these macaroons so much that I gladly make them without that excuse, though. They are heady with chocolate and gorgeously chewy and, all in all, dangerously addictive. Luckily (or not, depending on your point of view here) they are quick and easy to make.

> **2 egg whites**
> **1¹/₂ cups powdered sugar**
> **1 cup ground almonds**
> **3 tablespoons cocoa**

1 Preheat the oven to 400°F and line 2 baking sheets with baking parchment or preferably Silpat.

2 Mix the egg whites (unbeaten) with the powdered sugar, ground almonds, and cocoa until you have a sticky but cohesive mixture.

3 Fill a large bowl with cold water and dip your hands in it to dampen them before rolling the mixture into little balls the size of small walnuts. You will probably have to redunk your hands to keep wetting them as you go.

4 Arrange the macaroon-balls on the lined baking trays, leaving at least 2 inches between them, and put in the oven to bake for 11 minutes. It's hard to tell when they're ready, as they will seem squishy, but they harden up a little as they cool, and anyway, they should be damp within; that's what makes them chewy, so don't worry that the underneaths of the macaroons look sticky.

Makes about 25

There is something about the holiday season that seems to instill a piercing fear and quite unparalleled tremor of expectation in people. I can't quite work out whether the greater part is dread or hope — certainly there are components of both — but we seem to feel that for this crucial period we must suddenly become great hosts and untiring chefs, ready with a cocktail and a full table at all hours, at half an hour's notice. That is the kind of person we want to be — oh, and unstressed, smilingly organized, and unflappable too. Can this be arranged? Up to a point.

Strangely, this is not the hardest time of the year for the quick cook at all. Obviously, I can't make a turkey cook in under 30 minutes, but I have covered that great central feast at so much length before that I thought it wiser to concentrate on the satellite areas of stress and related culinary juncture points anyway. But I do have one quick tip for Thanksgiving dinner as I'm here, and it is as follows: Instead of making a stuffing for the turkey, buy some good sausage meat (or I use my favorite Cumberland sausages) from the butcher and using your hands, wiggle some space between the skin and the breast of the bird and squeeze the sausage meat in there. In other words, you're stuffing the top of the bird (beneath the skin) rather than inside it. Then cook it at top volume, so to speak. You can really blitz the bird, as the sausage meat stops the breast from drying out. Don't mean to boast, but I have got an 18-lb (and that's minus the weight of the sausage meat, mind) turkey cooked — in a 475°F oven — in two and a half hours.

But back to the job at hand: I want you to feel better about the big parties, the little dinners that you suddenly find yourself giving without having quite intended to issue the invitation, the meals you end up hosting for stray out-of-towners or distant relatives.

The main trick, if trick it really be, is to remember that abundance is the key. And the mood of welcoming plenty can be bought with relatively little effort. What would be tiring is to try and throw a party that aimed to be the night of a thousand canapés. My mantra has always been "a lot of a little rather than a little of a lot." In other words, choose what you want and make a lot of that, rather than dithering or feeling that you must provide a huge array and many choices, which will just multiply your labors and, in the end, because you'll have less of each, it won't look as cozily welcoming.

As in food, so in decoration. I don't like garishness, but I want warmth, and I take the tea-light route. This doesn't have to be expensive: I just put "votive candle" into the eBay search field and then batch-buy cheap. Once you've got a room dotted with red or pumpkin-colored shot-glass candle holders, each one alight, it doesn't matter if they cost next to nothing each; indeed it's better. And remember, even if each one looks hideous close-up, they will look fine en masse. It sounds strange, but that's true. Ugly flowers are the same: They work in abundance. Just think: A bunch of marigolds is hideous; a field of them, impressive.

And you've got an advantage with candles, as the light they give off is always beautiful. Not that I'm averse to Christmas lights, either. I love them everywhere so long as they're white and don't flicker. This time of year anyway invites excess, so don't worry about overdoing anything, and just go for it. The only thing that ruins a party is anxiety. But I'm not going to be so irritating as to tell you you don't have to worry: I'm giving you the recipes that will make you know you don't have to.

A LITTLE BIT OF THE HOLIDAY SPIRIT

I certainly don't think you need to offer a choice of drinks at a party, except that you must provide both for those who do and do not drink alcohol, but it's good to have a few seasonal cocktails in mind. The Snowball has fallen out of favor, I know, but it's a pity: It could hardly be more seasonal and tastes like grown-up ice cream soda, plus it's very much easier to make than eggnog. Christmas in a Glass is really what it is: The smell of the gingerbread syrup as the Prosecco's fizz spritzes it through the air is almost parodically festive. I use the French syrup (mentioned earlier in the book) that bartenders have decorating their shelves and I get it online, but now that there's a coffee shop at pretty much every corner, it's very easy to buy the gingerbread syrup they use to douse their lattes at this time of the year. As for the Pomegranate Bellini, this is just Prosecco (or other dry fizzy white wine of your choice) with pomegranate in place of peach puree. If you can't find the pomegranate puree (which, again, I buy online), then do substitute it with the 100 percent pomegranate you can find a little more easily: It's thinner and less intense, so maybe consider a dash of grenadine for a boost. Do not decorate with pomegranate seeds (choking hazard), but consider adorning the serving trays or bar area with pomegranate halves.

Finally, the Rouge Limonade, a drink that is considered not quite *comme il faut* in Paris, but much loved in the country. It is really just a spritzer made with red wine, only in place of club soda you use lemonade. Obviously, don't use good red wine — and this is why this can be a major help at a party. I don't say serve the sort of wine that could double as paint stripper, but something pretty rough could have its edges knocked off with a good top-up of lemonade. It's not chic, but it's thirst-quenching — and wonderfully, seasonally, hued.

SNOWBALL

Ice cubes
1 part Advocaat
3 parts chilled lemonade
Squeeze of lime juice to taste

1 Fill a highball glass with ice.

2 Add the Advocaat and then top up with the lemonade.

3 Spritz in the lime juice to taste.

One 70cl bottle (about 3 cups) of Advocaat should provide for around 14 Snowballs

CHRISTMAS IN A GLASS

4 parts chilled Prosecco or other fizzy dry white wine, well chilled
1 part gingerbread-flavored syrup

1 Pour the Prosecco into glasses.

2 Top with the scented syrup.

One 750ml bottle of Prosecco should yield about 5 glasses

POMEGRANATE BELLINI

1 part chilled pomegranate puree or concentrated juice
3/4 part chilled Prosecco or other fizzy dry white wine

1 Pour the pomegranate puree into a glass.

2 Top with the Prosecco.

One 750ml bottle of Prosecco should yield about 6 Bellini

ROUGE LIMONADE OR RED LEMONADE

3 parts chilled red wine
1–2 parts chilled lemonade

1 Pour the red wine into a glass or tumbler.

2 Top with the lemonade according to taste (and quality of wine), much like you would a white wine spritzer.

One 750ml bottle of red wine should yield 5 or 6 glasses

MARTINI OLIVES

A party has got to have bits to pick at, and what could be better than these? I got the idea of Martini Olives (without the martinis) from a colleague of mine from the *New York Times*, Denise Landis, from her lovely book, *Dinner for Eight*. These aren't just great to have at a party, they're mighty fine to stash in jars and give as presents.

4 8-oz jars pimento-stuffed green olives (this gives 4 cups)
$^1/_4$ cup gin (or vodka if you prefer)
1 tablespoon vermouth
1 teaspoon chile oil

1 Open the jars and drain the olives, putting them into a bowl with the gin, vermouth, and chile oil, and give them a stir.

2 Leave to steep for half an hour or so while you get ready for your party. You can put any you have left over in a jar with a lid for another couple of days, or indeed longer, though it's doubtful that will arise.

Makes 4 cups olives

MAPLE PEPPER PECANS

I cannot, just cannot allow myself to have even one of these as I'm setting them out, or I know there will be none left for the party. They're best eaten still a little warm (though be careful that they're not hot or everyone will have a burned mouth), though still very good cold and, as with the olives, make a good present, stuffed into a jar and tied with a ribbon or some such.

   I like the afterhit of fire you get from the cayenne pepper; if you want these to have a little more universal appeal, either reduce to $^1/_2$ teaspoon or substitute mild paprika.

4 tablespoons butter   **1 teaspoon cayenne pepper**
$^1/_2$ cup maple syrup   **3$^1/_3$ cups pecan halves**
1$^1/_2$ teaspoons table salt

1 Melt the butter with the syrup, salt, and cayenne pepper in a pan over gentle heat.

2 Add the pecans and stir to mix, then leave them on the heat for 2–3 minutes. Spread the pecans on a Silpat sheet or piece of aluminum foil to cool.

3 Arrange the sticky pecans in bowls to serve.

Makes 3$^1/_3$ cups

PARTY POPCORN

This is a very speedy, almost comedically so, party eat that is also, obligingly, rather thrifty to make (thus allowing for the extravagance of the pecans on page 319). It's really quite zingy and packed with flavor and might alarm any passing child expecting more regular sugary fare. I find that it's hugely popular, which is why I make a substantial batch of it.

2 tablespoons vegetable oil
1 cup (unpopped) popcorn
4 tablespoons butter
2 teaspoons ground cinnamon

2 teaspoons ground cumin
2 teaspoons ground paprika
4 teaspoons table salt
4 teaspoons sugar

1 Put the oil into the biggest pan you have with a lid over high heat, add the popcorn, and quickly put on the lid.

2 Let the popcorn pop, shaking the pan every now and then to keep the kernels moving. You will hear it, but don't be tempted to look, unless you want to get shot at, and once it has stopped popping — a couple of minutes or so — take it off the heat.

3 Melt the butter with the spices, in another pan, salt, and sugar, then pour it over the popcorn and put everything into a large paper shopping bag. Fold the top over to hold in the popcorn.

4 Shake, shake, and shake the bag again to mix the popcorn and get it thoroughly coated in the spicy butter.

5 Arrange in several party bowls.

Makes 12 cups

COCKTAIL SAUSAGES

If you want to have something hot to pass around on a tray, then cocktail sausages are what you're after. There's nothing fiddly to make, nothing to go right or wrong, and everyone loves them. These are not just any cocktail sausages: The sesame oil, honey, and soy give them a sweet-savory stickiness that is pretty well impossible to resist.

2¹/₄ lbs (75 in number) cocktail sausages
¹/₂ cup honey
2 tablespoons sesame oil
2 tablespoons soy sauce

1 Preheat the oven to 425°F.

2 Separate the sausages if they are linked and arrange them in a large, shallow roasting pan.

3 Whisk together the honey, oil, and soy sauce and pour over the sausages, then use your hands — or a couple of spatulas — to move everything around in the pan so that all the sausages are slicked.

4 Roast for 25–30 minutes; give them a shuffle about halfway through cooking if you happen to be near the oven.

Makes 75 cocktail sausages

Halloumi Bites

These are messy to eat — but then just about everything is so far — and are probably best as part of a table, rather than as a tray bound snack. If you have the pasta parked somewhere, perhaps sit this alongside. They go very well together, and eaters can fork up each easily enough. But I wouldn't count these out as finger food, so long as you dole out enough paper napkins. However, since the sausages probably make baby wipes a consideration anyway, I wouldn't worry unduly.

$1/4$ cup garlic oil

3 tablespoons chopped parsley

2 tablespoon lime juice

good grinding of pepper

3 8-oz blocks halloumi cheese, drained

1 Combine the oil, parsley, lime juice, and pepper in a large shallow dish.

2 Slice the drained halloumi into $1/4$-inch-wide pieces, and then cut each slice in half again. Don't worry if bits splinter as you cut.

3 Heat a dry skillet and dry-fry the slices of cheese until golden on both sides. This should take only a minute or so in a hot pan.

4 Put the fried halloumi into the shallow dish of other ingredients as you go, and then turn the halloumi about to coat each piece before turning into a serving dish.

Serves 10–12 as part of supper, more as a canapé

FESTIVE FUSILLI

You can think of this either as a soaking-up end-of-party meal for the hard core who manage to stay the course or a festive but unfussy supper you can get together quickly after some seasonal get-together or outing. The halloumi goes well for either occasion, but the pasta is definitely big and bold enough to be a stand-alone. Should you be lucky enough to have any left over, know that this is a superb post-party breakfast forked straight from a container in the fridge.

By "sunblush" tomatoes, I mean those ones that are halfway between fresh and dried and come soaked in seasoned oil from specialty and gourmet shops; it is their name, not mine.

4 cups sunblush tomatoes in seasoned oil	2 lbs fusilli or other short pasta of your choice
$1/3$ cup vodka	1 cup mascarpone cheese
2 teaspoons kosher salt or 1 teaspoon table salt	$2/3$ cup chopped curly parsley
2 teaspoons sugar	flaked Parmesan, to serve

1 Put a huge pot of water on to boil for the pasta.

2 Take out about 1 cup of the tomatoes and chop them finely. I use my mezzaluna here, as you can really mulch them.

3 Put the chopped sunblush tomatoes into a bowl with the other tomatoes, along with the vodka, salt, and sugar. Leave them to steep while you cook the fusilli.

4 Cook the pasta according to the package instructions, then drain and put back in the pan with the mascarpone, mixing well over low to medium heat.

5 Tip in the tomato mixture and half the chopped parsley, mixing well together.

6 Pour into a bowl and sprinkle over the remaining parsley. Serve with the Parmesan.

Serves 10–12

SEAFOOD POT

In France and Italy, and across much of Europe, seafood is traditionally eaten on Christmas Eve and it is a very good way of embarking on the meat feast that is to follow. But you don't have to stick to the custom, just keep this in mind for a very quick, warming, and yet elegant supper. A fennel salad before or after would be lovely, but you need no more than just some bread to dunk with. Adding the Holiday Hot Cake (see page 344) as a dessert would finish the evening off with gusto, and in suitably festive fashion.

1 lb 10 oz cherrystone or littleneck clams
1 lb 10 oz monkfish fillet
1 lb 10 oz salmon fillet
1 lb 10 oz cleaned squid
2 tablespoons butter

drop of vegetable oil
$^1/_2$ cup white wine
$^1/_4$ cup Pedro Ximénez or other rich dark sherry
2 tablespoons chopped chives, optional

1 Soak the clams in a bowl of cold water, leave them for about 5 minutes while you slice the fish, then discard the open or cracked clams and drain the rest.

2 Cut the fish into $^1/_2$-inch slices, and also slice the squid into the same width rings.

3 Melt the butter and oil in a large pot or pan with a lid, then over high heat toss in the fish and squid and stir them around until they begin to go opaque.

4 Add the clams and white wine, and clamp on the lid, shaking the pot over the heat, and let it cook for about 3 minutes.

5 Lift the lid, avoiding the steam, and pour in the sherry. Cover again and leave for another 3 minutes or so, shaking about again every now and then.

6 Serve the seafood in the pot, sprinkling over the chopped chives, if preferred.

Serves 6–8

BROCCOLI AND STILTON SOUP

At this time of year, it's good to have a thick warming soup at your fingertips and this is plenty seasonal into the bargain. This is what makes it easy: I make it from frozen broccoli; I use frozen organic broccoli, if that makes you feel any better. Actually, there's no reason to feel bad on any count. This is better when made with frozen, as well as making it more convenient as an impromptu standby. The broccoli is frozen fresh, whereas the drooping heads at the bottom of my fridge inevitably end up brassy and brassic. Moreover, at this time of year my fridge is too full as it is, and I need the help of having some crucial ingredients stashed in the freezer.

This is also a helpful way of turning plain cold sliced turkey into a warming meal.

3 tablespoons garlic-infused oil
6 scallions, finely chopped
$2^1/_4$ lbs frozen broccoli
2 teaspoons dried thyme
5 cups hot vegetable stock (from concentrate or bouillon cube)

$1^1/_2$ cups crumbled or chopped Stilton cheese
freshly ground pepper
1 long red chile pepper, deseeded and finely chopped, optional

1 Put the garlic oil in a large pan over medium heat and add the sliced scallions, cooking for a couple of minutes.

2 Add the frozen broccoli and thyme and stir on the heat for a minute or so.

3 Add the hot vegetable stock and the crumbled Stilton and bring to a bubble, then clamp the lid on and cook for 5 minutes.

4 Liquidize in a blender (or failing that, a food processor) — in batches — then pour back in the pan and heat if it has cooled too much while liquidizing; add pepper to taste.

5 Scatter with a Christmas confetti of red chile dice on each serving, if you feel like it.

Makes 9 cups, enough for 4 as a supper or 8 as a starter

Butternut Squash with Pecans and Blue Cheese

This has many strings to its bow: It serves as a vegetarian alternative to the Thanksgiving turkey; it gussies up a plate of cold leftover turkey; it adds the right balance of mellow warmth and tang to any plain wintry dish; it is a good whole meal on days when you just feel fleshed out.

4$\frac{1}{2}$ lbs butternut squash
3 tablespoons olive oil
6 stalks fresh thyme or $\frac{1}{2}$ teaspoon dried thyme

1 cup pecans
1 cup crumbled Roquefort or other blue cheese

1 Preheat the oven to 425°F.

2 Halve the squash, leaving the skin on, and scoop out the seeds, then cut into 1-inch cubes; you don't need to be precise, just keep the pieces uniformly small.

3 Put into a roasting pan with the oil and strip about 4 stalks of thyme of their leaves, sprinkling over the butternut squash. If you can't get any fresh thyme, sprinkle over dried. Roast in the oven for about 30–45 minutes or until tender.

4 Once out of the oven, remove the squash to a bowl and scatter over the pecans and crumble over the cheese, tossing everything together gently.

5 Check the seasoning and add the last couple of stalks of thyme, torn into small sprigs, to decorate.

Serves 6–8

TURKEY TONNATO

This is a seasonal version (and speedier to boot) of the Italian *vitello tonnato*: Instead of poaching veal and then making mayonnaise with tuna, I fan out some slices of cold turkey, left over from the feast, onto a plate and quickly whiz up the tuna mayonnaise using really good tuna — the one I use comes in a jar and is from the belly of the beast, called "ventresca." Even though my mother's shade would curse me for buying "fresh" mayonnaise rather than making my own, that's what I do here. I wouldn't want any white gloop out of a jar, though.

This is gorgeous with a wintry salad of shredded radicchio; the bitterness offsets the richness of the pinky-buff–colored mayonnaise dressing. If you've got time, a hot baked potato alongside is also, strangely, good.

1 cup fresh mayonnaise, from a specialty shop or gourmet store	4 teaspoons lemon juice
1 cup drained best-quality tuna	1–1$^1/_4$ lbs cold sliced turkey breast
$^1/_3$ cup sour cream	8 anchovy fillets, each cut in half lengthwise
$^1/_2$ teaspoon paprika	1 tablespoon drained capers

1 Put the mayonnaise, tuna, sour cream, lemon juice, and paprika into a blender, and whiz to make a sauce.

2 Arrange the turkey slices on a large platter, and then pour over the tonnato sauce to cover most of the turkey slices.

3 Arrange the sliced anchovy fillets in a crisscross pattern, or however pleases you, and scatter the capers about on top as well.

Serves 6

SPICED PEACHES

For me, this is an absolute Holiday Must and, as with so many good things in my life, comes to me from my sister-in-arms, Hettie Potter. I've used jarred peaches, I've used canned peaches, and it honestly doesn't matter which, but I'm afraid you have to resist the healthier peaches canned in fruit juice rather than syrup. If you can find only slices, not halves, so be it. This is a beautiful condiment to eat with roast ham, hot or cold, and I love it with cheese, too. It makes the kitchen feel like a proper holiday kitchen — and it's a very easy present to whip up for people, too, beautiful in old-fashioned glass jars.

2 14-oz cans peach halves in syrup
1 tablespoon rice vinegar or white
    wine vinegar
2 short cinnamon sticks
1^1/$_2$-inch piece fresh ginger, peeled
    and sliced thinly into rounds

^{1}/$_2$ teaspoon crushed dried chiles
^{1}/$_2$ teaspoon kosher salt or ^{1}/$_4$
    teaspoon table salt
^{1}/$_4$ teaspoon whole black peppercorns
3 cloves

1 Empty the cans of peaches into a saucepan with their syrup.

2 Add the vinegar, cinnamon, sliced ginger, chiles, salt, whole peppercorns, and cloves.

3 Bring the pan to a boil, and let it boil for a minute or so, then turn off the heat and leave it in the pan to keep warm.

4 Serve the peaches with a hot ham, letting people take a peach half each and some of the spiced juice. Any leftovers can (and should) be stored in a jar and then eaten cold with cold ham.

Serves approx. 8 people with a ham roast

CHOCOLATE PISTACHIO FUDGE

I am willing to believe that a confectioner wouldn't call this proper fudge, but it tastes divine, and you won't need a sugar thermometer or have to test for frightening soft or hard ball stages. I like this best made slightly less express, but with no greater effort, by stashing it in the deep freeze. It goes really grainy and fudgy this way. If I'm not handing this straight round at a party or with coffee after dinner, I might keep half in my freezer, and put the other half in a box or two for Christmas presents. Make sure they stay cold, though.

12 oz semisweet chocolate, chopped
1 14-oz can condensed milk
pinch of salt

1 cup shelled pistachios
2 tablespoons butter

1 Melt the chopped chocolate, condensed milk, butter and salt in a heavy-bottomed pan on low heat.

2 Put the nuts into a freezer bag and bash them with a rolling pin until broken up into both big and little pieces.

3 Add the nuts to the melted chocolate and condensed milk and stir well to mix.

4 Pour this mixture into a 9-inch-square aluminum foil pan, smoothing the top.

5 Let the fudge cool and then refrigerate until set. You can then cut into small pieces approximately 1³/₄ by 1³/₄ inches in size. Cutting 7 x 7 lines in the pan to give 64 pieces best achieves this.

6 Once cut, you can keep it in the freezer, no need to thaw; just eat right away.

Makes 64 pieces of rich fudge

QUICKLY SCALED MONT BLANC

This is a pared-down, lazy person's Mont Blanc, the traditional dessert of chestnuts, chocolate, and cream. Think of it as gastro-geography: Crumbled chocolate is the soil; chestnut puree the mountain; cream the snow; the final scattering of meringue, fresh snowfall. Sounds whimsical, but when something tastes like this you don't care about anything else.

I cannot have too much chestnut at this time of year, and please consider doing a variant of the Nutella Pancakes on page 374, replacing the Nutella with sweetened chestnut puree and the Frangelico liqueur with rum. You could substitute some broken pieces of marrons glacés for the chopped hazelnuts, but you could just as easily leave them out altogether.

4 oz semisweet chocolate
2 cups heavy cream
2 meringue nests (approx. 3 inches in diameter each), from a packet
1 1-lb can sweetened chestnut puree or spread, such as Clement Faugier

1 Chop the chocolate with a mezzaluna, sharp knife, or in a food processor until you have rubbly shards. Divide the chocolate among 6 smallish glasses — with about $^1/_2$ cup capacity.

2 Lightly whip the cream, and crumble and fold through one of the meringues.

3 Dollop the chestnut puree or spread, on top of the chocolate rubble. Then spoon over the cream and meringue mixture, crumbling a little more meringue over the top of each one.

Serves 6

MINCEMEAT PARCELS WITH BOURBON BUTTER

This is not a time of year when you want to forget the sweet stuff, and this is a fabulous, fast-forward mince pie. You buy a couple of packages of ready-rolled puff pastry, unfurl one sheet, dot with mincemeat, cover with the other unrolled sheet and stamp out squares with a small fluted cutter. Then they go into the oven (though they could sit in the fridge first, were that to be helpful to you). If you have some left over after they've been cooked, don't worry, just reheat them in a 350°F oven for about 15 minutes.

They do spill out like accordions sometimes on baking, but they just need to be pressed back into shape, which is both easy and satisfying. Oh, and the bourbon butter is not an optional extra: It is a reason for living in and of itself. All you do is cream 1 stick butter with 1 cup packed soft light brown sugar in a mixer, processor, or by hand, and gradually beat in 2–3 tablespoons bourbon, to taste. I've made a lot, because it's very good to have around at this time of year, and not just on Christmas cake or pudding. It's also worth bearing in mind for spreading over any sort of fruit that you might want to blister under a hot broiler. Or it may profitably be eaten straight from a spoon.

One 17.2-oz package (two 9^1/$_2$ x 9^1/$_2$-inch sheets) ready-rolled puff pastry, thawed if frozen
^{1}/$_3$ cup superior mincemeat
1 egg

1   Preheat the oven to 425°F. Carefully unfurl the pastry sheets and lay them out flat.

2   Using a 1^1/$_2$-inch-square cutter (ours was fluted), outline lightly (don't cut through) one of the sheets with squares covering the pastry and lining them up neatly in a grid with no gaps

3   Put scant ^{1}/$_2$ teaspoons of mincemeat into the middle of each square.

4   Beat the egg and then with your finger, outline the edges of the squares with an eggy line.

5   Cover the sheet of pastry with the other sheet, placing it directly on top. Press down at the edges, and then run down the sides of each square with your fingers to form a rough outline of bumpy filled squares.

6   Using the cutter again, this time cut right through the pastry to make ravioli-type parcels. Make sure they are sealed at the edges before placing the parcels on a baking sheet spaced slightly apart.

7   Bake for 15 minutes. As I mentioned, they are likely to open out like accordions, but don't panic. Once out of the oven you can squeeze them gingerly back together with the golden lids on top.

8   Let them cool on a rack to a bearable warm before serving with the bourbon butter.

Makes 35

HOLIDAY HOT CAKE WITH EGGNOG CREAM

This is a holiday-spiced version of those magic pudding cakes, which look like some sort of joke as you make them, pouring boiling water over batter, but when they've been cooked, turn out to be admittedly unhandsome cake with thick sauce underneath. Looks are not everything, and the ginger-butterscotch flavor of cake and sauce makes this a seductive winner. And that's even before we've gotten to the eggnog cream. This is a miracle topping that you will want to put on Christmas pudding, hot chocolate, any cake or pie, or in fact anything and everything. I see no earthly reason why not to.

2 cups water
1 cup flour
1$^1/_2$ cups light brown sugar
1 teaspoon baking powder
2 teaspoons ground ginger

2 teaspoons pumpkin pie spice
$^1/_2$ cup whole milk
$^1/_4$ cup vegetable oil
1 egg
6 teaspoons butter

1 Preheat the oven to 425°F and place a baking sheet on the oven shelf. Put the water on to boil.

2 Mix the flour, $^1/_2$ cup of the sugar, the baking powder, 1 teaspoon of the ground ginger, 1 teaspoon of the pumpkin pie spice, the milk, oil, and egg together.

3 Put into a greased 9-inch round baking dish about 2$^1/_4$ inches deep.

4 In another bowl, mix together the remaining cup of sugar with the remaining teaspoons each of ground ginger and pumpkin pie spice, and sprinkle over the batter in its baking dish. Dot the butter over the batter and pour over the boiling water. Trust me.

5 Put on the baking sheet in the preheated oven for 30 minutes. Let stand for 10 minutes before serving, and make sure you scoop out the sauce beneath the cake in the dish.

Serves 6–8

EGGNOG CREAM

1$^1/_2$ cups heavy cream $^1/_2$ cup Advocaat

1 Put the cream and Advocaat in a bowl.

2 Using an electric mixer, whip until thick but still soft.

3 Serve with the holiday hot cake, or indeed any festive dessert.

Makes approx. 2 cups

MARSHMALLOW CRISPY SQUARES

You'd think this was designed to keep the children happy, and while that's OK with me, adults find it particularly irresistible. But if you can't appeal to the child within at this time of year, when can you?

If I can find a tub of edible disco glitter in one of my cupboards, I sprinkle some on while the marshmallow is still sticky, but it has a certain pearly, luminescent appeal as it is.

It's also beautiful cut into squares and pierced, each piece with a white birthday-cake candle and arranged on a stand. Alternatively, you could turn this into more of a pickable treat, by cutting the slab into teeny-tiny squares so people can pop one straight into their mouth.

> 3 tablespoons butter
> 6 cups mini marshmallows
> 6 cups crispy rice cereal
> edible glitter or sprinkles, optional

1 Melt the butter in a large saucepan over low heat.

2 Add the marshmallows and cook gently until they are completely melted and blended, stirring constantly.

3 Take off the heat and immediately add the cereal, mixing lightly until well coated.

4 Press the mixture into a greased 13 x 9-inch pan; you may have to put on latex gloves and press it down into the corners, as it will be very sticky. Flatten the top and then sprinkle over the edible glitter or sprinkles if so inclined.

5 Let the marshmallow crispy squares cool completely in the pan and then cut them into 24 squares.

Makes 24 squares

STEEPED CHRISTMAS FRUITS

I suppose this is the lazy person's Christmas pudding, only that makes it sound like some sort of also-ran, and it is in actual fact rather more of a reward for the time-squeezed and exhausted. Well, we deserve one. I always used to steep dried fruits in brandy, then I moved on to rum, and now I'm firmly settled into a period with Pedro Ximénez. If you haven't ever tried this rich, dark, raisiny sherry, then I beg of you, do so. And although the suggestion of dolloping dry fruits steeped in it is already a shortcut, I can offer an even shorter shortcut, which is simply to pour this sherry straight over some vanilla ice cream for an instant, perfect dessert.

My sister Horatia and I have a strict no-presents policy for Christmas (our birthdays are both right after) and giving her a jar of liqueur-steeped fruits like this is my way of getting around the ban.

5 cups mixed luxury dried fruits (a mixture of raisins, sultanas, currants, and candied cherries)
1³/₄ cups Pedro Ximénez sherry, or other rich dark sherry, plus some

1 Tip the dried fruit into a 6-cup preserving jar, or use many smaller jars.

2 Pour in the Pedro Ximénez; the liquid will more than cover the fruit, and over time the fruit will swell with the sherry, growing to fill the jar.

3 Leave the fruits for at least a week, although if you were desperate overnight would just about do. In either case, just make sure you keep topping up with sherry as the liquid gets absorbed.

4 Eat with vanilla ice cream, or however you want.

Makes 6 cups

SEASONAL FRUIT SALAD

This time of year quite reasonably enough has me foraging about my déclassé drinks cabinet. I've already found very good use for my Advocaat and now I can't help reaching for the Tuaca. This is a Tuscan liqueur, ultra-Christmassy, rather like a sweet brandy with vanilla and orange; think panettone in liqueur form. I don't expect everyone to keep some at home, though I bought mine easily enough (too easily some might say) and there would be worse things than having this around the house just for drinking during the festive season. But you can replace it with a mixture of brandy and Cointreau or some sweet sticky orange liqueur if that's easier. I wouldn't rule out just plain brandy, but if you use it, double the sugar when making the syrup.

As with the steeped fruits on page 348, the *Express* point of this isn't that it can be all done and dusted in five minutes flat — some longer steeping is advised — but that it is NO EFFORT WHATSOEVER. This always matters, but it matters now more than ever.

6 satsumas or clementines
1 cup Tuaca, or a mixture of brandy and Cointreau

$^1/_2$ cup sugar
$^1/_2$ cup pomegranate seeds

1 Peel the satsumas or clementines and put the segments into a bowl.

2 Pour over the Tuaca and leave for a couple of hours or overnight.

3 Drain the fruit, and then put the sugar into a small pan with the Tuaca. Stir to dissolve the sugar, and then bring to a boil and do not stir again at all, but let it boil for 5 minutes.

4 Let the syrup cool slightly, and then pour back over the satsuma or clementine segments. Add the pomegranate seeds and tumble to mix.

Serves 6–8

HOT TODDY

Although it's true this is the season of goodwill, it is also the season of colds and chills, and so it is only fair to end with something to take the edge off and generally de-sniffle and uplift.

¹/₄ cup bourbon (or rum if you prefer)	**1 teaspoon lemon juice**
¹/₄ cup water	**small paring of lemon zest**
1 tablespoon honey	**1 clove**

1 In a small pot, pour the bourbon, water, honey, and lemon juice and put on the heat.

2 Pare a shaving of lemon zest, stud with a clove, and drop in the pan.

3 When everything's warm, pour into a glass and drink.

Serves 1

I get a sense that everyone believes there to be some secret pantry rules that, once applied, mean you never have to go shopping again and can cook anything and everything without a moment's thought. It just isn't so, and couldn't be so. What all recipes have in common is that you have to go shopping for them, and whether the ingredients required are recondite or uninspiringly everyday, doesn't make a difference. That is stating the obvious, but I feel it's necessary.

Of course, you can keep an awful lot on hand, and I do. But you have to maintain a balance between having enough food to keep you from having to go shopping every day, but not so much that your cupboards are sagging with the weight of cans you hardly ever need. As someone who has a terrible hoarding instinct, I know how useless a full cupboard can turn out to be.

For the truth is, you don't want a diet made of food that can be kept indefinitely. And even if you did, it wouldn't be good for you. I like to know that I've got the wherewithal to make pasta and sauce for the children without a shopping expedition; I like to know that if I buy a roasting chicken, I've got some white beans to mash, along with the garlic or truffle oil to turn it from blah to brilliant; I like to know that if someone drops in unexpectedly, I can construct some sort of dessert I had no plan to cook hitherto, but any more and I fear I am not filling a pantry but building a bunker.

I can certainly give an indication of what I think's helpful to keep on hand; most of these ingredients have already made their presence felt throughout the book. After all, it's impossible to have so many quick and easy recipes without a great deal of reliance on the pantry on an everyday basis.

Most of my shortcuts involve infused oils, with garlic-infused oil in top position and vegetable oil suitable for a wok the next most regularly used, chile oil coming in third, but still most definitely earning a place on the podium. I am lazy enough to be happy to buy them, but if you want to make your own, it's not hard. For 2 cups of regular olive oil, chop up 8 garlic cloves and let it all steep for 48 hours before straining into a bottle (with a funnel, or you'll waste your precious work); so that's the garlic oil. For the oil I like to use for wok or other quick cooking, don't use olive oil but rather $1^3/_4$ cups sunflower or other vegetable oil, $^1/_4$ cup of toasted sesame oil, 4 sliced cloves of garlic, and a 2-inch piece of sliced ginger strained after the 48 hours' steeping; for chile oil, use 2 cups vegetable oil and chop up 4 hot red chiles, and let them sit, seeds and all, in the oil before straining after the 48 hours as with the other oils. You can pretty well flavor any oil as you wish, and although you don't, strictly speaking, have to strain out the bits, as so long as they are immersed in oil, they shouldn't go off; I find it easier to do it at the beginning than have to think about it again.

I always keep a barrage of beans and other legumes in the house: This means I have the wherewithal for a vegetable, a starter-salad, a soup or protein for non-meat eaters. I think it's important to use the freezer as an extension of the pantry, too. And I don't just mean as a repository of prepared dishes that can be thawed, but for as many vegetables as possible. Don't sniff: The vegetables in your deep freeze are likely to have far more nutrients than the veg lying hopefully at the bottom of your refrigerator.

I could go on, but I don't want to be prescriptive about what you should or could keep in your fridge and on your shelves, as just written as a list, it's largely unhelpful. But the recipes that follow provide honest guidance as to what I think can get you out of a jam when you've got people to feed on little or no notice. Good luck!

My Three Favorite Dressings

It's not hard to make a dressing every time you want a salad — and there's nothing wrong with just a spritz of lemon, a shake of salt, and a drizzle of fabulous oil straight onto the leaves in the bowl — but I tend to keep my three most used, most loved shaken up in jars about the kitchen. I don't keep them in the fridge but no doubt the health and safety police would tell me I have to.

I use these not just for the obvious, but also as a good way of spritzing up plain boiled or steamed vegetables, and they can also serve as marinades, though I'd dilute with more oil rather than apply them straight in that instance.

Golden Honey Mustard Dressing

This is wonderful on any salad, but particularly good on bitter leaves such as endive or radicchio. If you can't get rapeseed oil, the dressing will be less golden, but any oil of your choice will do.

$1/4$ cup Dijon mustard

2 tablespoons honey

$1/3$ cup lemon juice

1 cup rapeseed oil

1 teaspoon kosher salt or $1/2$ teaspoon table salt

Put all the ingredients into a jam jar, make sure the lid's on firmly, and shake like mad.

Makes 1 cup

Anchovy Red Wine Dressing

Again, this is good on robust bitter leaves, but acts as a glorious contrast to the soft sweetness of grilled peppers. I keep packages of char-grilled peppers in the freezer, which I roast from frozen and then douse in this.

8 anchovy fillets

$1/4$ cup red wine vinegar

$1/4$ cup garlic-infused oil

$3/4$ cup olive oil

1 Put all of the ingredients into a blender, and whiz to make the dressing.

2 Pour into a jam jar and put on the lid to store.

Makes 1 cup

WASABI LIME DRESSING

This beautiful green dressing packs a real punch: I love it on watercress and avocado salad and, indeed, on anything that is served with something fairly plain, when you welcome the buzz.

3 tablespoons lime juice
1/4 cup peanut oil
1 tablespoon wasabi paste from a tube
1/2 teaspoon kosher salt or 1/4 teaspoon table salt

Put all of the ingredients into a jam jar, and again shake to mix, remembering to put the lid on firmly first.

Makes 2/3 cup

RED PEPPER HUMMUS

You know those days when you had no idea you were having people for dinner and then that phone call comes midafternoon? Well, this is the quickly assembled first course that can turn a plain roast chicken or anything else you think you can stretch for four people without much effort, into a dinner party. And actually, whenever you have to cook without time for planning, I think a roast chicken is nearly always the main course you need: It's much easier to come up with frills for before and after and alongside than to construct a fancy dinner party dish at the last minute.

This can be dolloped onto crostini (and you can buy baby toasts ready made for the purpose in Italian markets) or eaten as a dip and it even serves as a rather intriguing, gorgeously hued sauce for plain grilled meats.

1 14-oz can chickpeas	1 teaspoon lime juice
1 12-oz jar roasted red peppers	1 teaspoon paprika
2 tablespoons cream cheese	salt
2 tablespoons garlic-infused oil	

1 Drain the chickpeas and peppers and put them into a food processor.

2 Add the cream cheese, oil, lime juice, and paprika.

3 Whiz to a hummus-like puree, and then add salt and perhaps more lime juice according to taste.

Makes 2 cups

GOLDEN GOAT CHEESE

It's always worth keeping your own bread crumbs around (I have bags of them in the freezer) but I am a total convert to the way of panko, which is the Japanese bread crumb mix you can buy in packages and then, once opened, leave in the freezer to use just as they are; you never need to thaw them.

What makes this recipe a real pantry standby is that the little discs of fresh goat cheese, which come vacuum packed, have an unbelievably long use-by date, so you can keep them for emergencies and bring out something really very impressive when the occasion demands.

If you fry the crumb-coated cheese it will go a deeper gold, but the oven method requires less of you; it's your choice.

1 egg
good grinding of fresh pepper
$^1/_2$ cup panko bread crumbs
4 1-oz rounds of fresh goat cheese

1 Preheat the oven to 425°F.

2 Beat the egg in a wide bowl with the pepper, and put the bread crumbs into a wide shallow dish.

3 Dip the goat cheese in the peppery egg and then press into the bread crumbs firmly. You will need to turn the cheese over and press on the other side to coat evenly; press a little on the sides as well.

4 Sit the breaded goat cheese on a baking sheet and cook for 10 minutes, by which time the cheese will have become gooey inside but will still hold its shape. You can also fry these, in which case, heat a pan with enough oil to nearly cover the cheeses as they fry. Once the oil is hot, they will only need a minute or so on each side. Drain on paper towels.

Makes 4

LENTIL AND WALNUT SALAD

There is no need to serve this with the goat cheese, but the pairing certainly makes for a special starter without too much ado.

1 14-oz can organic Puy lentils
(ready cooked)
$^1/_2$ cup walnut pieces
$^1/_4$ cup chopped chives

4 teaspoons walnut oil
2 teaspoons sherry vinegar
$^1/_2$ teaspoon kosher salt

1 Drain and rinse the lentils and put them in a bowl with the walnuts and chives.

2 Whisk together the oil, vinegar, and salt, then dress the salad, stirring well and checking the seasoning.

Serves 2 or 4 with the goat cheese

SALADE NIÇOISE

Everyone seems to have a very strong opinion as to what should or should not go into a salade niçoise, so let me tell you from the outset, I have no desire to enter the fray. I put in what I have at home from, broadly, the accepted canon, but not necessarily everything. Since the tomatoes we get mostly don't have a lot of flavor, I tend to use those tubs of slightly embarrassingly named "sunblush" tomatoes and their intense, flavorful acidity works well here. I am a great believer in keeping these on hand.

Otherwise, speed being of the essence, the only real deviation here is that I use croutons (some high-end baked ones from a package will do) rather than boil some potatoes and then have to wait for them to cool.

If any recipe demonstrates what you can make almost exclusively from pantry ingredients, then this must be it.

2 eggs, preferably organic	4 teaspoons extra virgin olive oil
1/2 cup frozen green beans	juice of 1/2 lemon
1 cup sunblush tomatoes in seasoned oil	1/2 teaspoon sugar
1/2 cup sliced pitted black olives in brine	1/4 teaspoon kosher salt or pinch of table salt
8 cups torn iceberg lettuce	1 cup croutons
1 8-oz jar or can excellent tuna, about 6 oz drained weight	4–6 anchovy fillets — or indeed none, to taste
	1/2 cup fresh basil leaves

1 Put the eggs in a panful of cold water, bring to a boil, and let boil for 7 minutes. Three minutes in, add the frozen beans.

2 Drain the beans and eggs, and let the eggs sit in a bowl under running cold water. Put the beans in a strainer and hold under the tap for a moment or so. The eggs and beans stop cooking and the beans get cold.

3 Tip the tomatoes and their oil into a bowl, add the olives, and mix gently.

4 Put the lettuce on a serving dish and then top with the tomato-olive mixture, saving their flavorsome oily juices in the bowl for the time being.

5 Drain the tuna and place chunks with the tomatoes and olives, then strew the salad with the drained beans.

6 Using the tomato mixture's oil that has been left in the bowl, make the dressing: Whisk in the olive oil, lemon juice, sugar, and salt to make an emulsion and pour over the salad.

7 Peel and quarter the almost but not quite hard-boiled eggs and add to the salad along with the croutons, the anchovy fillets, and the basil.

Serves 2 for supper or lunch

MINESTRONE IN MINUTES

This is child's play to make, and I use the term advisedly, since it is the invention of my ten-year-old son Bruno (Brunostrone, we call this soup at home) and we make versions of it constantly. Use any beans or legumes you want, or a mixture is good, too, and you can play with the pasta sauce as well. If you're coming down with a cold (and no child is eating this), I suggest you use the spiciest, hottest sauce you can find.

While I've got you, let me just give you a quick outline of another fast soup, excellent for children's supper and much beloved *chez moi*. We call it easy risi e bisi, as it's a simplified version of the Venetian risotto-like soup using rice and peas; here goes: Put 4 cups of vegetable stock in a pan with 1 cup frozen peas, $1^1/_2$ cups of risotto rice, and 1 oz shaved, crumbled, or grated cheese (of any sort); let it come to a bubble, and then simmer with a lid on for 20 minutes. At the end, I have to admit that I remove the lid and stir in 2 4-oz jars of 100 percent pea baby food (Beech-Nut Tender Sweet Peas to be precise) and then ladle it into bowls with more cheese if any child wants.

This is even faster.

1 14-oz can mixed beans (sometimes sold as mixed bean salad) or other canned beans

3 cups hot chicken or vegetable stock

1 cup tomato-based pasta sauce of your choice

4 oz ditalini or other soup pasta

1 Drain the beans and put them into a saucepan with the hot stock and pasta sauce.

2 Bring the pan to a boil and then add the ditalini, cooking according to package instructions.

3 Once the pasta is tender, switch off the heat, remove the pan to a cool surface, and let stand for 5–10 minutes if you can bear to wait. The pasta swells in the soup and everything just gets better.

Serves 2–3

MERGUEZ WITH HALLOUMI AND FLAME-ROASTED PEPPERS

This is another easily assembled sausage dish, but slightly lighter all told. Not that it wouldn't fill up a tableful of hungry eaters, but nothing can compete with sauerkraut for putting hairs on chests, and that sort of general bolstering.

I keep packages of halloumi cheese on perpetual standby in my fridge, and the peppers I keep in jars in the cupboard. But you could always use a pack of frozen char-grilled peppers that you had prepared. Indeed, if you slice them thinly enough, you can use fresh bell peppers. Merguez is my spicy sausage of choice here, but chorizo has a longer fridge life if that's a consideration. Anything you can buy vacuum-packed can only help here, too.

8 merguez or spicy sausages (approx 12 oz)
1 8-oz block halloumi cheese
1 8-oz jar roasted peppers
1 tablespoon garlic-infused oil

1 Preheat the oven to 425°F. Put the sausages into a low-sided roasting pan (this makes the cooking time quicker).

2 Slice the halloumi into $1/4$-inch slices and then lay them on and around the sausages in the pan.

3 Take the peppers out of the jar and also strew them around the sausages and cheese, cutting them into smaller slices and pieces as you go, then drizzle over the oil.

4 Cook for 15–20 minutes, by which time the sausages should have browned and the cheese colored in places.

Serves 4

CURRY IN A HURRY

This is such a favorite fallback of mine, I would never be without the staples I need to make it: coconut milk and green curry paste in the cupboard; various packages of green vegetables in the freezer. Of course, there are the other bits and pieces, too, but these are the main ones. The chicken thigh fillets I buy as and when I need them.

If you want to make this with fresh vegetables rather than frozen, then up the water (keeping the amount of stock the same) and indeed I would double it to 2 cups. This is what to cook when you find out midafternoon that you've somehow acquired 6 people for dinner.

2 tablespoons canola or other vegetable oil

3 tablespoons finely chopped scallions

3–4 tablespoons green Thai curry paste

2¼ lbs chicken thigh fillets, cut into strips about 1½ inches by ¾ inch

1 14-oz can coconut milk

1 cup boiling water

enough chicken stock from bouillon or concentrate to make 2 cups

1 tablespoon fish sauce

1½ cups frozen peas

1½ cups frozen soybeans

1½ cups frozen slender beans

3 tablespoons chopped fresh cilantro

cooked rice or noodles, to serve

lime wedges

1 Heat the oil in a large saucepan, one that owns a lid, and drop in the scallions. Cook, stirring for a minute or two, and then add the curry paste.

2 Add the chicken pieces and keep turning over heat for 2 minutes before adding the coconut milk, stock (or rather water and chicken bouillon or concentrate), and fish sauce, and then the frozen peas and soybeans.

3 Simmer for 10 minutes, then add the frozen beans and cook for another 3–5 minutes.

4 Serve with rice or noodles, as wished, sprinkling over the cilantro as you do so. Put a plate of lime wedges for people to squeeze over as they eat.

Serves 6

MELLOW MEATBALLS

This recipe uses many of the same standby ingredients as the chicken curry, but what it makes tastes very different. I buy organic beef mini-meatballs from the supermarket, which makes this extremely easy to get together, and there'd be nothing to stop you freezing them and cooking them right from frozen if that helps. Though in that case, I'd just pop them in hot sauce and not attempt to brown them first.

Sure you can make your own meatballs, but so long as you're happy with the origin of the meat (which is always, always important), don't beat yourself up about cutting out a stage when you know everyone's going to be happy come suppertime. Likewise the package of diced veg: Once everything's swimming in its mellow sauce, no one's going to be asking questions.

It's just a case of making life easier on yourself; frankly, no one else is going to.

3 tablespoons red curry paste
2 tablespoons vegetable oil
40 organic mini meatballs (1 lb 5 oz in weight)
1 teaspoon ground ginger
1/2 teaspoon ground cinnamon
1 14-fl oz can coconut milk
1 14-oz can chopped tomatoes
1 14-oz can chickpeas, drained

12 oz diced butternut squash and sweet potato (in a package from supermarket)
2 cups chicken stock from bouillon cubes or concentrate or from a package
2 tablespoons honey
cooked rice, to serve
1/2 cup chopped fresh cilantro

1 Heat the curry paste and oil in a large wide pan, and when it starts sizzling add the meatballs, turning them in the red oily mixture.

2 Sprinkle over the ginger and cinnamon and fry the meatballs for a couple of minutes.

3 Add the coconut milk, chopped tomatoes, and drained chickpeas. Stir in the diced squash and sweet potato and then the stock and honey.

4 Bring the pan to a boil, and then simmer for 20 minutes. Serve with rice and then decorate each plate with some chopped cilantro.

Serves 4–6

Sausages with Sauerkraut

The choucroute garnie I wrote about many years ago in *How to Eat* took several hours to make and included much anointing with goose fat — and very good it was, too. Truth to tell though, I don't believe this to be any less good and I may be as surprised as you are to find it in a chapter on pantry items. But it makes sense: The sauerkraut is preserved in jars or in refrigerated plastic bags, and the sausages are smoked and I keep a supply of them in my deep freeze. But that's only because I order them frozen; when I buy smoked sausages from the specialty shop or butcher, I let them live happily in the fridge.

It may seem extravagant to use a whole bottle of wine to cook it all in, but it's touches like this that elevate simple ingredients. And remember: It's the quality of the wine that leaves its note on this whole dish.

This is very, very good with a pan of plain steamed potatoes alongside and this really isn't any work for you.

5¹/₂ cups sauerkraut, rinsed in cold water and drained

8 smoked sausages, cut into smaller lengths if wished (approximately 2¹/₂ lbs)

2 teaspoons juniper berries

3 dried bay leaves

1 750ml bottle Riesling wine

1 teaspoon white peppercorns

1 Preheat the oven to 400°F. Cover the bottom of a small to medium roasting pan with the drained sauerkraut.

2 Add the sausages, juniper berries, and bay leaves.

3 Pour over the wine and sprinkle over the peppercorns.

4 Bring the pan to a boil on top of the stove, then cover with aluminum foil and cook in the oven for 30 minutes. Serve with steamed potatoes if you wish, and definitely some German beer mustard.

Serves 6

CHOCOLATE PEAR PUDDING CAKE

This is a cross between pears belle Helene and Eve's pudding, but that's an irrelevance really. The only important thing to remember is that this is easy, quick, and very comforting and seems to please absolutely everyone. It's not hard to make sure you always have what you need in the house to make this. And for hot days when baked cake and sauce seems inappropriate, then bear in mind that canned (or jarred) pears and chocolate sauce — with or without vanilla ice cream — make a lovely dessert on their own.

You can make the chocolate sauce on page 51, or buy one you like, obviously, but I have a complete pantry standby of a sauce I make by heating together 3/4 cup evaporated milk, 1/2 teaspoon instant espresso powder, 1/2 cup dark corn syrup, and 3 1/2 ounces semisweet chocolate.

The cake itself does make a little bit of its own sauce, so if you really don't want to make some separately, just serve with chocolate ice cream.

As with any baking, you really do want all ingredients at room temperature before you start.

2 14-oz cans pear halves in juice	1 teaspoon baking powder
1 cup plus 2 tablespoons sugar	1/4 teaspoon baking soda
3/4 cup plus 1 tablespoon flour	2 eggs
1/4 cup cocoa	2 teaspoons vanilla extract
10 tablespoons (1 1/4 sticks) soft butter plus more for greasing	

1 Preheat the oven to 400°F and grease an 8 1/2-inch-square ovenproof dish with butter.

2 Drain the pears and arrange them in the base of the dish.

3 Put all the remaining ingredients in a processor and blitz till you have a batter with a soft dropping consistency.

4 Spread the brown batter over the pears, and bake in the oven for 30 minutes.

5 Let stand for 5 or 10 minutes and then cut into slabs — I cut 2 down and 2 across to make 9 slices — and serve with chocolate sauce.

Serves 6–8

NUTELLA PANCAKES

Let joy be unconfined. This is the one of the most irresistible desserts I think I have ever made, and I did it by no more than some fruitful scrimmaging about my cupboards. I long for it almost constantly, and it is not good that it is so easy to make, not good at all.

If you don't run to Frangelico yourself — and there is no reason why you should — then simply replace this hazelnut sticky liqueur with some rum. And incidentally, I love this as much when made with sweetened chestnut puree (though it's so strong, you could use much less) in place of the Nutella. In which case, I definitely use rum, and forgo the chopped hazelnuts altogether, dotting either with a few crumbled marrons glacés as a special treat, or some chocolate sprinkles.

8 store-bought crepes
1¹/₂ cups Nutella
6 tablespoons soft butter
¹/₃ cup plus 2 tablespoons Frangelico

¹/₃ cup chopped hazelnuts (from a package)
1 cup heavy cream

1 Preheat the oven to 400°F.

2 Put each crepe in front of you and spread some Nutella over one half and then fold the unspread side over the spread side. Now add a dollop over one quarter and fold again, so what you have is a fat, squidgy fan. Place in a buttered jelly-roll pan or similar. Proceed with the remaining 7 crepes, overlapping them a little in the pan as you go.

3 Put the butter in a small pan with the ¹/₃ cup of Frangelico and heat to melt the butter.

4 Pour over the crepes in their dish, sprinkle over most of the chopped hazelnuts, and bake in the hot oven for 10 minutes.

5 Meanwhile, whisk the cream with the remaining 2 tablespoons of Frangelico until you have an aerated soft floppiness and put into a bowl, sprinkling with the last of the chopped hazelnuts. This luscious cream is a must alongside the sweet, buttery, heavenly crepes.

Serves 6–8

CLAFOUTIS

A traditional clafoutis, from the Limousin region of France, is *tout court*, a baked custardy batter filled with cherries. The cherries, moreover, are not stoned, which I think has very little to commend it, save ease of execution. My version is even easier: I use morello cherries (they must be sour to be a contrast to the sweet eggy batter) out of a jar, one or two of which are all at times to be found somewhere (usually the back) of my cupboard.

Whereas the traditional Limousin pudding is baked slowly so that you have a soft, flan-like custard, I blitz mine brutally so it is more like a cherry-studded Yorkshire pudding. I've given the bare bones for my larder standby; but since I keep quite a crammed drinks cabinet too, I often add $1/4$ cup of Kirsch to mine, reducing the amount of milk to 1 cup. The sweet-toothed might like to add two more tablespoons of superfine sugar to counter the boozy hit, but I don't.

If you haven't got a tarte tatin dish handy (though I use mine for so many recipes, including roasting small birds, I can't recommend one too highly), use an 8-inch pie dish or solid cake tin.

2 teaspoons vegetable oil	$1/4$ cup Kirsch, optional
$1/2$ cup flour	2 cups drained morello cherries from
$1/4$ cup sugar	a jar
4 large eggs	$1/2$ teaspoon powdered sugar (optional)
$1^1/4$ cups 2% fat milk	

1 Put the oil in a copper tarte tatin dish or any shallow solid cake tin or pie dish of about 8 inches diameter and put the dish in the oven, preheating it to 450°F as you do so.

2 In a large bowl, mix the flour and sugar and then whisk in, either by hand or using an electric mixer, the eggs, one by one, the milk, and the Kirsch, if using. Remember to reduce the milk to 1 cup if you use the Kirsch.

3 When the oven beeps to show it's reached the required temperature, or however else it deigns to let you know, stir the drained cherries into the batter, quickly open the oven, take out the hot dish, pour the cherried batter in, and pop it quickly back into the oven.

4 Bake for 30 minutes, by which time the sides will be bronzed and puffed, rising dramatically away from the edges of the tin, though it subsides pretty well immediately after it's come out of the oven, so the moment of pleasurable triumph is fleeting. Ah well.

5 Let stand for about 10 minutes (20 is fine, too, and it is addictive cold, too), then dust with powdered sugar just before serving, if the fancy takes you.

Serves 6–8

VANILLA APPLES WITH SWEETHEART CROUTES

This is what I make when I was not expecting to have to make a dessert and have nothing around and no time to be clever. I grab the apples from the fruit bowl — I've specified Gala, but really, use whatever's at hand — and take some slices of the children's plastic sliced white bread. And you know what? This really works. Everyone's fooled, even me. In an ideal world I'd like a bit of thick pourable cream with it, but if there isn't any, I'm not complaining.

4–6 tablespoons butter
2 Gala apples
2 tablespoons vanilla extract

3 slices of bread, cut into heart shapes
    with a cookie cutter
sugar, for sprinkling

1 Melt the butter in a skillet, reserving a spoonful for later.

2 Finely slice the apples (don't bother to peel or core; curiously I get about 22 slices out of 2 apples, don't ask me how) and add them to the pan, cooking for about 3 minutes, then add the vanilla and cook for about another 5 minutes total, turning once.

3 Remove the apples to a plate, then add the remaining spoonful of butter to the pan and quickly fry the sweetheart croutes.

4 Arrange the sweetheart croutes on the plate with the apples and sprinkle with sugar. Serve with cream if you've got some.

Serves 4

STORECUPBOARD SOS

ACKNOWLEDGMENTS

As I draw this book to an end, I conclude that I am extraordinarily fortunate in owing so many people thanks. The drawback is only that a long list requires an unwonted and unwarranted terseness. The china, linen, cutlery and general embellishment in the photos that precede this come from my own cupboards and an almost dangerous eBay habit, but on top of that I am grateful to the following: Absolute Flowers; Baileys; Cabbages & Roses; Ceramica Blue; The Cloth Shop; The Conran Shop; The Cross; The Dining Room Shop; Divertimenti; Gelateria Valerie; Habitat; Heals; Le Creuset; Liberty; OKA; Petersham Nurseries; Something...; Summerill & Bishop; Thomas Goode.

I couldn't have produced these recipes without the food, delivered in almost comical amounts, by Allen's, James Knight, Michanicou Brothers and Panzer's.

Fiona Golfar, long-standing friend and überstylist, provided most of her furniture and also Rose Murray, my Second-Hand Rose, who in turn threw herself into the book, and my chaotic life, with charm and hard work, a winning combination.

I am grateful to Elinor Klivans and her publishers Chronicle Books, San Francisco, for permission to reprint her recipe for Totally Chocolate Chocolate Chip Cookies from her book *Big Fat Cookies*.

As ever, I am indebted, heartswellingly so, to Hettie Potter and Zoe Wales, my life-support system, who brought this baby into the world with me, as did Caz Hildebrand, whose instinct, wit, brilliance, unfailing eye and generosity are constantly invaluable to me. I am grateful to Francesca and Lisa Grillo, Anzelle Wasserman and Kate Bull for their support; without their work, I could not do my work. I feel extraordinarily blessed in my publishers, and want particularly to thank Poppy Hampson, Gail Rebuck, Alison Samuel, Will Schwalbe and Leslie Wells (and their backroom support teams, including Jan Bowmer and Mary Gibson). I am aware, too, of my good fortune in coming across Lis Parsons; her photographs provide just the pictures I dreamt of for my recipes.

It would be wrong, too, for me to fail to acknowledge my stepdaughter Phoebe, and my children Mimi and Bruno without whom this would be pointless.

To Ed Victor, my agent and friend, inordinate amounts of love: this is for you.

For Charles: thank you, thank you, thank you.

INDEX

NIGELLA EXPRESS